Sandy Jeffs OAM has published eight volumes of poetry and a memoir *Flying with Paper Wings: Reflections on Living with Madness*. In 2020 Sandy and co-author Margaret Leggatt published a book about Larundel Psychiatric Hospital, *Out of the Madhouse: From Asylums to Caring Community?* which won the Oral History Prize at the 2020 Victorian Community History Awards. Much of Sandy's writing has been about her life with schizophrenia for which she has been the public face for many years. Sandy lives in Christmas Hills in the Yarra Valley.

Also by Sandy Jeffs

Poems from the Madhouse (1993, 2000, 2002)
Loose Kangaroos (co-author, 1998, 1999)
Blood Relations (2000)
Confessions of a Midweek Lady: Tall Tennis Tales (2001, 2009)
The Wings of Angels: A Memoir of Madness (2004)
Flying with Paper Wings: Reflections on Living with Madness
(2009, 2010, 2016)
Chiaroscuro (2015)
The Mad Poet's Tea Party (2015)
Out of the Madhouse: From Asylums to Caring Community?
(co-author with Margaret Leggatt, 2020)
The Birds of Eltham
(co-author with photographer Tony Robinson, 2020, 2021)

The POETICS of a PLAGUE

A HAIKU DIARY

The 2020–2021 COVID-19 Pandemic

SANDY JEFFS

First published by Spinifex Press, 2021

Spinifex Press Pty Ltd
PO Box 5270, North Geelong, VIC 3215, Australia
PO Box 105, Mission Beach, QLD 4852, Australia

women@spinifexpress.com.au
www.spinifexpress.com.au

Copyright © Sandy Jeffs, 2021

The moral right of the author has been asserted.

All rights reserved. Without limiting the rights under copyright reserved above, no part of this publication may be reproduced, stored in or introduced into a retrieval system, or transmitted, in any form or by any means (electronic, mechanical, photocopying, recording or otherwise) without prior written permission of both the copyright owner and the above publisher of the book.

Copying for educational purposes
Information in this book may be reproduced in whole or part for study or training purposes, subject to acknowledgement of the source and providing no commercial usage or sale of material occurs. Where copies of part or whole of the book are made under part VB of the Copyright Act, the law requires that prescribed procedures be followed. For information contact the Copyright Agency Limited.

Edited by Susan Hawthorne and Pauline Hopkins
Cover design by Deb Snibson, MAPG
Typesetting by Helen Christie, Blue Wren Books
Typeset in Adobe Garamond
Printed and bound by CPI Group (UK) Ltd, Croydon, CR0 4YY

 A catalogue record for this book is available from the National Library of Australia

ISBN: 9781925950366 (paperback)
ISBN: 9781925950373 (ebook)

For Jackie who has taught me so much about being a writer, Margie who constantly amazes me and Anne who inspired a young, ever-grateful high school student to embrace the world of ideas.

Acknowledgements

These poems could not have been written without the love and support of Robbie and Dido who, during the lockdown, were a constant source of amusement, strength and practicality. It was their suggestion that I keep this diary. Our COVID haven in the bush was a place of peace and quiet where the lockdown was felt much less harshly than in Melbourne's inner city and suburbs. It gave me the space and mental stillness in which to create these haikus. This was an absolute privilege. Thank you to Veronica who suggested the wonderful title. Thank you to Susan and Renate for publishing this labour of love and to all at Spinifex for your continuing support over many years. And thank you to Pauline and Susan for your close and detailed editing of this idiosyncratic book. I commend Spinifex for their ongoing commitment to publishing poetry.

The Story So Far

Before the plague days, Australia's year from hell began with the 2019-20 Black Summer bushfires which burnt an estimated 18.6 million hectares of bushland and pasture across many of the country's states. The worst hit regions were in New South Wales, which had experienced a prolonged drought, and East Gippsland in Victoria. Following this devastation, came floods in places that had been ravaged by fire. Australia was reeling from these unprecedented natural disasters with many fire-affected towns and their businesses struggling to recover. When the pandemic struck, it was another stake into the hearts of these towns and their people.

Meanwhile in the USA, the Trump presidency, into its fourth year, was continuing to be a sideshow. Trump had reinvented a politics with no rules and he had paid no heed to conventions. The White House became a soap opera that was compulsive viewing —like watching daily episodes of *Days of Our Lives*.

On 12 March 2020, the World Health Organisation (WHO) officially declared COVID-19 a pandemic. On Friday 13 March, Prime Minister, Scott Morrison, and Australia's Premiers and Chief Ministers, announced that mass gatherings—events with more than 500 participants—should not take place from Monday onwards. They also announced the establishment of a National Cabinet to respond to the coronavirus crisis. A level three travel warning was placed against the whole world, with Australians told to avoid unnecessary international travel. This was the beginning of Australia's response to the COVID-19 pandemic. Australia had 156 cases.

On 18 March, the *Ruby Princess* cruise ship arrived in Sydney harbour. The next day at 6 a.m. health officials gave the all-clear for the 2,700 passengers aboard the cruise ship to disembark. About 110 had influenza-like symptoms. Three were swabbed, but the rest were not made to wait for the results. They went home, many boarding domestic flights to other states, carrying the virus with them. Within five weeks at least 662 passengers on the *Ruby Princess* tested positive to COVID-19 and 21 died.

The restrictions imposed on people's movements affected many aspects of our social and working lives. Progressively, festivals and shows were cancelled. Anzac Day commemorations were cancelled. Restrictions were placed on visiting aged-care facilities. Gatherings were further limited. Australia's borders to overseas visitors were closed. Australians abroad were urged to return home as soon as possible. People over the age of 70 were advised to effectively self-isolate, as were people with chronic disease or comorbidities who are over the age of 60, and Aboriginal and Torres Strait Islander peoples over the age of 50. The Federal Government swung into fiscal policy mode announcing financial assistance for workers in various sectors of the economy. They introduced JobSeeker—a doubling of the Newstart unemployment income to $1100 per fortnight—and JobKeeper which was $1,500 per fortnight—a package to allow eligible businesses to keep paying their workers.

In Victoria, Premier Daniel Andrews had declared a State of Emergency on 16 March. The aim was to 'flatten the curve'. Stage 3 restrictions were introduced with residents only having four reasons to leave home—see below. Gatherings were further limited. Social distancing was encouraged. These measures seemed to be working and things were looking brighter. The National Cabinet moved forward its decision on easing restrictions to Friday 8 May. "We need to restart our economy. We need to restart our society. We can't keep Australia under the doona. We need to move ahead," the Prime Minister said. Accordingly, Stage 3 restrictions were eased in Victoria.

However, after a steady rise in new cases in June and July in Victoria, things started to spiral into a serious situation. A second wave of the virus was unfolding. The curve wasn't flattening. In light of the escalating number of new cases, and deaths, on the 7 July the Victorian government made the decision to enforce tougher rules and reintroduce Stage 3 restrictions coded

Lockdown 2.0. It was Groundhog Day. On 19 July wearing a face mask was made mandatory. These Stage 3 restrictions were to last for six weeks.

The Federal Government's mantra had been we're all in this together but with this lockdown, Victorians in general and Melburnians in particular, felt very much alone, an island within an island.

The Poetics of a Plague begins with Lockdown 2.0 as it affected me and my fellow Melburnians and regional Victorians. The rest of Australia is part of the haiku narrative. As is the wider world. It also documents Donald Trump who looms larger than life as he leads a troubled and destabilised USA into an election which is widely looked upon as a desperate battle for the soul of America.

What is coronavirus?

Coronavirus disease (COVID-19) is an infectious disease caused by a newly discovered coronavirus. Most people who fall sick with COVID-19 will experience mild to moderate symptoms and recover without special treatment. The virus that causes COVID-19 is mainly transmitted through droplets generated when an infected person coughs, sneezes, or exhales. These droplets are too heavy to hang in the air, and quickly fall onto floors or surfaces. You can be infected by breathing in the virus if you are within close proximity of someone who has COVID-19, or by touching a contaminated surface and then your eyes, nose or mouth.

Stage 3 Restrictions

There are only 4 reasons to leave home:
- Shopping for food and supplies
- Exercise
- Medical care
- Work and education if necessary

What will close:
- All businesses currently closed under Australia's Stage 2 restrictions
- All shops selling non-essential goods
- Hairdressing salons and most beauty service providers
- Schools: Prep–Year 10 students in metropolitan Melbourne and Mitchell Shire will begin Term 3 with remote learning from Monday 20 July until at least 19 August. Only VCE, VCAL and students whose parents and carers cannot work from home, and those attending local specialist schools, return on-site.

What won't close (for now):
- Corner shops and newsagents
- Vet surgeries
- Agricultural supply shops
- Dry cleaners
- Hardware shops
- Petrol stations
- Grocery stores
- Banks and pharmacies
- Some outdoor sporting facilities
- Food courts within shopping centres will only be able to sell takeaway. Shopping centres themselves will remain open.

Victorians will no longer be allowed to gather in groups of more than two for their household group, however Premier Daniel Andrews stated in his announcement that the return to Stage 3 measures would come with a few strings attached.

From Daniel Andrews

You will be able to go out to go to work if you have to, to go shopping for the things you need when you need them, to study, to provide care or to get care. People are well acquainted with those rules.

Daily exercise will be treated differently. You can't leave metropolitan Melbourne to get your daily exercise. There's a number, on the advice of the chief health officer, of very low public health risk activities that will be permitted that were not permitted last time but the most important point to make around exercise is that you can't be going on a four-hour bushwalk hundreds of kilometres away from Melbourne.

You can't be going fishing outside the metropolitan area, down into regional Victoria. Regional Victoria has very, very few cases and vast parts of regional Victoria have no cases. This is designed to keep it that way. I hope very soon to be able to be before you again talking about further easing of restrictions in regional Victoria. That's not for today. I do hope that is quite soon. And we'll only be able to achieve that if we continue to contain the virus within metropolitan Melbourne and not see large outbreaks or additional cases in regional Victoria.

Lockdown 2.0

....

Stage 3 Restrictions

Declared by Premier Daniel Andrews on 7 July
to begin at 11.59 p.m. on 8 July

Day 1 – 9 July

165 cases, 0 deaths

Back to Square One
Pandemic worsens,
Premier Andrews forced to act,
restrictions back on.

Stage 3—We Were So Hopeful
We were so hopeful,
thought the worst was behind us.
Yep, pie in the sky.

Long Road
A long road ahead
as we're confined to barracks.
What projects to do?

42 Days and Counting
Counting down the days
trying to create some Zen
mindful daydreaming

so, pass the popcorn
while I settle in to watch
the horror movie.

Chrissy Hills Asylum
Some places are hell
but we're lucky to be in
a country retreat

yes, an oasis,
a sanctuary and a haven—
our own asylum!

Patience
is such a virtue
when the days ahead seem long
but time *will* roll on.

Haiku OCD Meditation
Making the words fit,
fingers on the move counting
all the syllables

it's an Obsessive
Counting Disorder that is
uncontrollable

words broken into
their parts—it's meditative—
form and content meld.

Day 2 – 10 July

288, 0

Not Going Well
Over two hundred
cases of COVID out there,
we are all at risk.

North Melbourne Towers Lockdown
Towers in lockdown,
COVID cases climb too high—
poor buggers caught out.

Pessimism Chasm
Deep pessimism
begins to grip my thinking,
when will it all end?

Second Time
The second time round
doesn't inspire much hope that:
we can get through this.

My COVID Project
What am I to do?
Mend my violin bowing, my
technique needs some work.

'Unprecedented'
Words fail to describe
this pandemic's destruction
of our daily life.

A Haiku a Day Keeps
the black dog at bay,
poetry is my lifeline,
words enrich my day.

Day 3 – 11 July

216, 1

Pressure Builds
Dan under pressure,
cases are escalating,
people unhappy.

Politics of Fear
Pollies start blame game,
a dangerous game to play
when people suffer.

Just Lucky
Who would want to be
premier in a pandemic?
Poor Daniel Andrews.

Even ScoMo
I even feel for
ScoMo, our COVID PM,
who's steering the ship.

Trump's Fairyland
America reels—
thousands upon thousands die.
Trump in fairyland.

Brazil
Brazil in same boat.
Bolsonaro denies all,
meanwhile thousands die.

Day 4 – 12 July

273, 1

Days of Our COVID Lives
Days bleed into days,
not much difference between them.
COVID ennui strikes.

Cases Rise
Over 12 million
cases world-wide. Who will lead
us out of this mess?

Shrinking World
My world is shrinking,
the world beyond our house is
too grim to endure.

Shut My Door
Want to shut my door
and keep the bleak world at bay,
give me my bubble.

Day 5 – 13 July

177, 0

Not Good News
The news not so good,
cases are still far too high,
not out of the woods.

Shadow
A new world order.
We live in the shadow of
Coronavirus.

NSW
New South Wales alert,
pub cluster outbreak worry—
high moral ground lost.

Meanwhile in the USA
Florida surges
with thousands of new cases
and deaths to follow.

COVID Politics
Democrats wear masks,
Republicans refuse to.
COVID politics.

Interlude—Friends on the Move
More friends on the move,
another place beckons them—
feeling abandoned!

Day 6 – 14 July

270, 2

Crisis
Vic. virus crisis,
cases into stratosphere,
grim virus tally.

The Signs
The signs are not good,
people are flouting the rules.
So, what will it take?

Not Much Happening
Not much happening—
day after day after day
after day after

Joyful Small World
Joy's watching a blade
of grass quiver in the wind,
my life's so small now.

Leadership
Jacinda Ardern
shows the way with leadership—
trumps Trump any day.

Warning
WHO is warning world
the virus will get much worse,
governments must act.

Topsy Turvy World
Topsy turvy world,
US politics shambles,
lack of leadership.

Day 7 – 15 July

238, 1

Happy Birthday
Pandemic birthday,
no celebrations for me
while world is on edge.

Getting Older
The years are mounting,
edging to three score and ten—
counting every day.

Just Another Day
Birthday day, ho hum, ho,
just another COVID day—
same old, same old, same …

AFL to Relocate
AFL desperate—
teams will be relocating.
Vic. teams to Queensland.

Day 8 – 16 July

317, 2

Worse by the Day
It's getting worse by
the day. Over 300.
I watch on with fear.

Virus Runs Riot
Virus runs riot
embedding itself in our
defenceless bodies.

More Deaths in Victoria?
As infections grow
and hospitals treat the sick,
there will be more deaths.

Hope
I slept fitfully,
as dire as the world is—
morning—the sun rose!

COVID Black Hole
Book published, high hopes,
then along comes pandemic—
book into black hole.

What Now?
I wonder, what now?
Will the world be the same post
plague? I can't presume.

Mounting Deaths
Brazil, USA
breaking records every day,
the deaths are mounting.

Day 9 – 17 July

428, 3

Update
Vic. virus update,
I wait with trepidation,
how many today?

Biggest Yet
Crisis gets much worse.
428
biggest increase yet.

Deadly Virus
The deadly virus
is moving at breakneck speed,
how can we stop it?

Language
Pandemic language
uses institutional
words such as 'lockdown'.

My Big Day
Shower, breakfast, walk,
emails, haiku diary, then
play fiddle, watch box.

Book Therapy
Dive into a book,
immerse myself in ideas,
characters and verse

a beautiful way
to escape reality
and understand it.

Empty Diary
My diary's empty,
no appointments, no fun things,
nothing pencilled in.

Haiku World
Words circle my head,
the whole world's one big haiku
as I keep counting!

Day 10 – 18 July

217, 3

The News for Victorians Today
is a bit better,
217
a sigh of relief.

Fight of Our Lives
Jenny Mikakos,
the minister, warns we're in
the fight of our lives.

War
As cases increase
the battle for Vic. is a
national concern.

Purge the Virus
Group of physicians
urge workforce should be sent home
to purge the virus.

Prisons
Coronavirus
detected in a prison,
fears of it spreading.

Ready
ICUs ready,
medics on edge as risks rise,
they're at the coalface.

Questions Asked
Who's really in charge?
Questions about Dan's control
and what has gone wrong.

Stage 4?
Stage 3 lockdown now
to fight deadly pandemic.
Will there be stage 4?

Fashion Statement
Face masks essential,
designer masks all the go—
a fashion statement?

The Prof Says
Chief Health Officer
Prof. Sutton says: *everything
is on the table.*

Rising Toll
Nursing home clusters,
healthcare workers infected,
and deaths, raise concerns.

Language #2
Language has become
more about battling a war
than a health crisis.

The World is Waiting
The world is waiting.
Tests for vaccines underway
as we hold our breath.

237,743 in One Day!
WHO reports a surge
in the global number of
infected people.

Day 11 – 19 July

363, 3

Up Again
After yesterday
363
more cases again.

Rollercoaster
Vic. rollercoaster,
cases, up, down, up, down, up,
bumpy road ahead.

How are We Going?
Still not going well.
Victoria in the grip
of something deadly.

Face Masks Mandatory
Government says we
now have to wear a face mask
when away from home.

Fine
Things are serious,
a $200 fine
for not wearing mask.

NSW
Transmission risk high,
people are too complacent—
learn from Vic's mistakes.

Interlude — Climate Crisis
What climate crisis?
We have almost forgotten
there is a problem.

Because COVID has Sucked
the oxygen from
everything else in the world,
nothing else matters.

The Economy
Now for the bad news,
*our record unemployment
is worse than it looks.*

Shambles
Trump's US shambles,
train wreck response to COVID
with no leadership.

Day 12 – 20 July

275, 1

275 – Today's Tally
We watch the tally
like hawks—how many new ones?
It is wearying.

So Far to Go
Four months of lockdown
and we have so far to go.
I want it to end.

Stalker
Death toll is mounting,
600,000 world-wide—
the virus stalks us.

Friendships
Friends are kept apart
testing how close friendships are.
Will they survive this?

Team Sandy
Team Sandy tested,
COVID has taken away
some vital pieces

no gypsy music,
no hockey, no CHOPS, no chance
to visit my friends.

World Wide
Gone from bad to worse,
pandemic's skyrocketing
out of our control.

Interlude – Sleepless in Chrissy Hills
Bed's a battlefield,
my thoughts fly like butterflies
while sleep evades me.

Cluster Threat
Not out of the woods.
New South Wales cluster threatens,
virus is spreading.

Vic. Hotel Bungle
Hotel quarantine
bungle is perhaps the source
of the COVID spread.

Interlude – Celebrity Hubris
Rapper Kanye West
is running for President.
Misguided celeb?

Policies are thin,
messages from God saved him,
rambling rally speech.

Mad World
The world gets madder,
politics and COVID clash,
mad men in control!

Cottage Industry
Long queues at Spotlight,
sewing machines selling out,
mask production lines.

Day 13 – 21 July

374, 3

We Watch Concerned
The sixteenth day of
triple figure increases.
We watch with concern.

Following USA
Now we're doing it,
politicising face masks
like the USA.

Daily Dose
What is our daily
dose of miserableness
going to be? Lots.

Interlude—Guilty Pleasure
Crack the Diet Coke,
pandemic guilty pleasure—
old habit resumed.

Pandemic Zeitgeist
Negativity,
pessimism, permeates
our sense of being.

Tally Watchers
We're tally watchers,
each day we await the news,
how many today?

Government Review
Government reviews
JobKeeper and JobSeeker
and cuts foreshadowed

welfare payment cuts
pathway into poverty—
heartless government.

Vaccine Race
Scientists reveal
promising signs for vaccine.
Yep, the race is on.

Day 14 – 22 July

484, 2

Blowout
COVID case blowout
almost 500 today.
I wonder: what next?

Tuning In
Tune into Premier
with COVID daily update,
grim face with grim news.

Record High
Pandemic mayhem,
infections reach record high.
Dan wags his finger.

Figures and Stats
Figures, graphs and stats
chart the spread of pandemic—
the numbers don't lie.

First Lockdown
was a novelty
people reassessed their lives
iso not too bad

novelty's worn off,
people are spooked and afraid—
there's no end in sight.

Headline
Another headline
and another COVID day.
Oh, for some good news.

Dragging On
Days drag on and on
and it's only day 14—
slowly, slowly, slow.

Reconstruction Plan
The ACTU
launch their reconstruction plan—
jobs for the workers.

Fallout
Pandemic trauma—
social and economic
fallout predicted.

High and Dry
Actors, musos and
those in the arts miss out on
government bailouts.

Because
Liberals hate artists,
cannot stand criticism
from feisty poets.

Panic Buying
Elastic panic—
people rushing to buy it,
in-demand product

on the other hand
at least we have toilet rolls
on the market shelves

panic buying them
was an act of lunacy
during first lockdown.

Coronacoaster
Constant ups and downs,
riding the pandemic wave,
where will it take us?

Mental Health Intact
Delusions circle
but my malicious voices
are under control.

How am I travelling?
Surprise, mental health intact—
better than I thought.

Interlude—Larundel Dreaming
Madhouse in my dreams,
cannot get away from it
such was its impact.

Cabin-Fever
Thought I would struggle
with cabin-fever and stress,
amazingly, no.

Are We?
The saying has been:
we're all in this together.
I wonder, are we?

Interlude—Changing World?
Predictions are that
neoliberalism may
wither on the vine.

Need
The need for money
drives people to work while sick
or waiting to hear

casualised workforce
are at risk from pandemic
since they need to work.

Different this Time
People do dumb things
out of their fear and worry
about the future.

The Curve Is
upwardly mobile.
How can we flatten this trend?
This pesky virus.

Day 15 – 23 July

403, 5

Devastation
Vic. devastation,
the toll rises, five more deaths,
such depressing news.

Sledgehammer
COVID-19 blues
hit me like a sledgehammer—
these horrible times.

Blows My Mind
Unbelievable,
magnitude of pandemic
blows my mind apart.

Bloody Joke
MSO players
are on JobKeeper for now,
what a bloody joke.

Left High and Dry
Arts industry is
decimated—no help from
the Lib. government,

artists left to rot,
their talents not recognised
by politicians.

Lucky Me
How lucky am I?
Pension, home, friends, distractions,
while others suffer.

Maybe I am not
angry with Dan because I
haven't lost a job,

my home, business or
income. I'm not indebted
to the banks, or can't

pay my landlord rent.
I can see why others would
be furious and

want to take the law
into their own hands. I am
so privileged, others

aren't so fortunate.
They need our care, empathy,
and understanding

and as lockdown rolls
on their anger will seethe as
will their frustration.

It can only lead
to mental health crises and
desperate cries for help

and social unrest
of disgruntled and civil
disobedience.

Does Not Care
Virus does not care
who it affects, young or old,
it kills anyone.

Home Workplace
Working practices
have changed a lot since COVID,
home now a workplace.

Bleak Times
Government revels
bleak economic figures—
worst since WWII.

On Watch
Now is not the time
to fall into psychosis—
on mental health watch.

Day 16 – 24 July

300, 7

Before the News
Quiet start to day
before the news gets too bad
and the truth hits us.

Shrinking Economy
Jobless rate to soar
as the economy shrinks—
numbers looking dire.

Leadership Needed
Climbing this mountain
an out of this world effort,
leadership needed.

Before the Pandemic
Life was so different
before the pandemic, now
nothing is the same

Despondency
Second lockdown brings
the winds of despondency
into our frail hearts.

Zombie World
It's a zombie world,
with people mesmerized by
the COVID nightmare.

Aged Care Deaths
Old people at risk,
rising death toll in aged care,
must look after them.

Aged Care System Collapse
Not enough workers,
aged care in fear of collapse
the AMA warns.

At Risk
Health workers fearful
for the health of their clients
who are at grave risk.

Impossible to Hope
Maintaining one's hope
amidst this awful crisis
is impossible.

Alone
I feel so alone
locked up in my pandemic,
melancholic mind.

COVID Waters
Working on myself
to keep my head above the
deep COVID waters.

Social Distancing
is keeping us safe
while keeping us all apart
but loneliness comes.

Mantra
Let's stay connected
the mantra from government.
Are we together?

15.4 million
World-wide cases climb,
the tally is staggering—
the horror of it.

The Home Front
Here in Chrissy Hills
the home front fires are burning—
safe in our haven.

Troops Called In
Dan enlists army,
troops called in to help the cause,
door knocking duties.

Pandemic Hoax
Some people are drawn
to the conspiracy that
pandemic's a hoax

there are no people
dying from the virus, no
bodies, no cases

it's fake news because
the media are spinning
us a web of lies.

Day 17 – 25 July

357, 5

Dysphoria
Anxious, dysphoric,
people sinking into hole—
there's no easy fix.

Example
New Zealand success,
Jacinda Ardern shows way.
So, what can we learn?

Routine Needed
Establish routine,
have something to do each day,
watch out for boredom.

COVID Cover
COVID a cover
for governments to bring in
draconian laws.

Longest Winter
As our COVID days
unfold, we are enduring
our longest, bitter

winter as the slow,
trailing days of deep unease
unsettle our minds.

Begin Again
Medical experts
urge US to shut down and
start over again.

Anniversary
Another milestone—
six-month anniversary
since COVID began.

Pariahs
Border restrictions—
Victorians pariahs,
nobody wants us.

Charity Precarity
Charities struggle,
volunteers falling away,
money woes increase

they are on frontline
helping people in crisis
when no one else will.

Interlude—Circus
Kanye West circus,
madman or prophet? Who knows?
Something not quite right.

Seroquel Dose
World is psychotic
needs a dose of Seroquel
to settle its nerves.

The Future
How can Australians
pandemic-proof their futures
and find decent jobs?

Aviation Industry
Who would want to fly?
Aviation industry
doomed to fall from sky.

What Next?
The State's directive,
masks effectively Stage 4.
What will Dan do next?

Trump Panicking
USA chaos.
Black Lives Matter protests surge.
Trump is panicking.

Disunited
Disunited States,
USA a broken land
and no longer great.

Cracks
Cracks are opening
in Trump's sad America—
an empire crumbles.

The USA—Turning on Itself
No more charisma,
exceptional no longer,
turning on itself.

Day 18 – 26 July

459, 10

More Vic. Deaths
Deaths escalating
but nowhere near USA—
yet still concerning.

Like Drowning
COVID victims speak—
they suffered frightening coughing.
It was like drowning.

Bleak Story
As infections rise
the faces behind the stats
tell a bleak story.

Real People Suffer
Effects of virus
more than just tallying stats—
real people suffer

make no mistake, it's
an unfolding tragedy
that affects us all.

Exposure
COVID shows lack in
home front manufacturing,
leaves us short of goods.

Macro Economics
Small government now
uses macro policies—
Keynes back in favour.

Cataclysmic Times
An apocalypse?
Daily records are broken—
cataclysmic times.

When It's Over
will I be the same?
Nothing is as it once was.
When it's over, what?

Listening to Science
Science at forefront,
data will drive decisions
but are we listening?

Health Workers
Health workers at risk,
many have been infected
by this cruel virus.

Checklist
Mental health checklist
Voices? Delusions? Sleep? Mind?
Controlled but fragile.

My mind teeters on
a dark precipice, holding
my demons at bay.

Plague Days
Existential angst,
lowering of the spirit—the
plague days are with us.

Shopping Habits
Changed shopping habits,
retail therapy online
is all the go now.

Binge Buying
Binge buying—chooks, pets,
seedlings, toilet rolls, sewing
machines, elastic!

COVID Cliché
The making of bread—
oh, so clichéd and passé,
fads that come and go.

Casualised Workforce
Virus exposes
casualised workforce costs and
insecure work.

Supply and Demand
Face masks all the go,
designer styles are in vogue—
prices inflated.

Reality Hits Trump
Trump discovers that
denial won't stop virus.
Reality hits.

Trump's World
Trump's world crashing down,
public opinion shifting,
the polls are not good.

News Not So Fake
Fake news not so fake.
Trump's denial—chickens are
coming home to roost.

USA COVID Elections
Presidential race,
election turned upside down,
COVID game changer.

Day 19 – 27 July

532, 6

New Threshold
A new threshold reached,
the numbers are disturbing,
very challenging.

Tragedies Everywhere
Families lose loved ones,
people will be affected
and people will die.

Imploring Us
Dan implores us to
follow the rules to keep us
safe from the virus.

Head in Sand
I've stopped watching Dan
and put my head in the sand—
don't want to hear news.

Going Backwards
The story so far—
everything's going backwards
the future unknown.

Fluctuating Mood
My mood fluctuates,
going from hope to despair—
shaky, unsettled .

Circus
People need a break.
AFL a distraction,
circus but not bread.

Spending Up Big
AFL spending
three million a week to keep
the circus going.

2020
started with a bang.
First the gong, then the book launch
before COVID struck.

We Had
the summer from hell
which destroyed so many lives,
then a pandemic!

Distant Memory
Bushfires. What Bushfires?
Black Summer fades into past.
COVID takes over.

4 a.m.
4 a.m. haiku—
sleeplessness and the long night,
sharks live in my mind,

spooks and phantoms reign,
all things exaggerated—
words are my comfort.

Lessons
Lessons to be learned—
young Victorians speak out:
it is serious.

The Masked Shopper
Shopping with face mask
cannot recognise people
no smiling faces.

Deeply Embedded
Dr Coatsworth says:
virus deeply embedded,
will take time to halt.

Bags of Contagion
Virus incubates,
seething bags of contagion
are roaming Melbourne.

Uni Crisis
Jobs decimated,
academics are at risk,
ivory-towers fall.

'Karen'
'Karen' makes a stand.
These privileged white middle-class
women defy law,

claiming human rights
and other spurious laws,
they hold fast their ground.

So
will I need to read
the Magna Carta before
shopping at Bunnings?

Consider Others
From Dan to 'Karen':
you are not being helpful
consider others.

Dangerous
Anti-maskers and
conspiracy theorists run
dangerous campaigns.

Soap Opera
Trump stars in soapie,
truth is stranger than fiction,
mouths agape, we watch.

Tracking
social transmissions.
Epidemiologists
study COVID's course.

Day 20 – 28 July

384, 6

Tally Falls
After horror high,
Victoria's tally falls
but no halt to deaths.

Strategy
Breakfast and a walk
trying to build a routine—
COVID strategy.

Haiku Magic
No inspiration,
no haiku magic today—
but wait, here they come!!

Calm?
Not much happening,
peace amidst the frenzied times,
calm before the storm?

Court Rules
Court rules against the
Black Lives Matter protestors,
good cause, bad timing?

Petty Politics
Michael O'Brien
continues to carp at Dan—
petty politics.

Aged Care Crisis
Aged care in crisis,
it's our critical challenge,
keeping the old safe.

Blame Game
Vic. Government blames
Fed. Government who blames Vic.
Government who blames …

Profit Driven
Private aged care out
for profits. Money the root
of poor practices.

Making Room
Hospitals cancel
non-essential surgery
to free up their beds.

What are the Chances?
Lockdown due to end
in three weeks. But chances are
highly unlikely.

Airline Passengers
Airline passengers
test positive to virus,
New South Wales alert.

Third Wave?
Second COVID wave
has wreaked havoc on us all.
Will a third wave come?

COVID Fatigue
has wearied our souls.
We are bombarded with so
much horrible news.

Interlude — Hockey
Hockey season gone—
I don't have a year to waste
because of my age.

More Cases
Florida cases
surpass New York's case numbers—
disaster ahead?

USA — Not Enough Resources
The so-called rich land
does not have the resources
to treat the numbers.

Grey's Anatomy
The idea that *Grey's
Anatomy* donated
equipment from their
set to some needy
hospitals, sounds laughable,
but is all too true.

'Death Panels'
Florida decree—
'death panels' decide who lives,
who's sent home to die.

USA COVID Puzzle
Half do not believe
and half are dead or dying—
never the twain shall …

Day 21 – 29 July

295, 9

Glimmer of Hope
A glimmer of hope,
case numbers fall a little—
comes on deadly day.

Crisis Gets Worse
Nursing homes crisis,
old folks dying from neglect
while the fingers point.

Desperate Times
Desperate times in Vic.,
government brings in army
to help nursing homes.

Home or Hell?
People dying in
homes riddled with the virus.
Home or hell we ask?

Mirror, Mirror
Mirror, mirror … who's
the most vulnerable of
us all? The old folks.

Deepening
Prof. Brendan Murphy:
there'll be more deaths every day
as the plague deepens.

Workers from Interstate
Dark times with aged care,
replacement workers shipped in
to staff nursing homes.

Challenges
Bushfires, climate change,
pandemic—challenges sent.
What's next? Judgement Day?

Interlude – Kookaburra Chorus
A morning walk with
a cappella chorus from
the kookaburras.

High Moral Ground
States vie for kudos.
Gladys can't take moral ground—
think *Ruby Princess*!

Interlude – Ross's COVID Funeral
A funeral online,
people sit apart on chairs—
the sad masked mourners.

How?
How did it happen?
It was well under control
but virus is smart.

Spreading Virus
COVID scare alert,
Queensland slaps its borders shut.
Vic. teens spread virus.

Dramas
My haikus are not
about calm bucolic scenes—
they're virus dramas!

Leechcraft
Trump extols virtues
of hydroxychloroquine—
peddling leechcraft crap.

New Favourite
Doctor Stella, the
'Deliverance Minister', is
Trump's new favourite Doc.

She casts herself as
a prophet and destroyer
of tempting demons.

Dr Stella Immanuel Says
a vaccine made from
DNA from aliens
takes away your faith.

And Endometriosis in Women
says the good doctor
is because they have dreams of
hard sex with demons.

Soapie
USA soapie—
caricature of themselves.
Yep, *Days of Our Lives*.

Day 22 – 30 July

723, 13

Death Surge
The news gets grimmer,
infections soaring, deaths surge—
record day again.

The Culprit
Family transmission?
Workplaces the culprit? Not
cafes, pubs, restaurants.

Outrage
Outrage at people
who delight in flouting rules,
it's disappointing.

Stupid
'Eve Black' who posted
on Facebook her outrageous,
arrogant, display

of dissent, when she
was stopped by police, has been
arrested by them.

Her disregard for
others could close businesses
or kill elderly.

Lying and Cheating
You can't account for
people lying and cheating
the authorities.

Crystal Ball
Looking ahead, but
the crystal ball is clouded,
has lost its power.

Can't Imagine
I can't imagine
thousands of daily cases—
hundreds are enough.

Restrictions Extended
Dan extends virus
restrictions to include more
shires and areas.

Interlude—Morning Walk
Purple pea flowers,
a beautiful sunny day,
the promise of Spring?

Stranger by the Day
Curiouser and
curiouser, the world gets
stranger by the day.

Unleashed
The pandemic has
unleashed weird and whacky types
who peddle untruths.

What price?
The curly question:
economy versus health—
what price for a life?

A New World
Data confronting,
adjusting to this new world
is not that easy.

Concerns in Qld, NSW
Queensland, New South Wales,
concerns for rising numbers,
borders an issue.

I Never Thought
I never thought I'd
find myself in the middle
of a pandemic.

The Bell Tolls
COVID misery,
infected and dying are
for whom the bell tolls.

Consequences
Three young women charged
by Queensland police for breach
of border controls.

They face hefty fines
or up to five years in jail
for deceitful ruse.

Outing of them has
sparked racism claims. They're of
African descent.

Tentacles
Virus tentacles
spreading beyond Melbourne's realm
regions under threat.

Doggie Power
Sniffer dogs will be
trained to detect the virus—
yap! Doggie power.

Oldism
If kindergarten
kids were dying like oldies,
imagine the fuss.

USA Election Race
Biggest threat to us
is what Trump is prepared to
do to win the race.

Chosen One
Evangelicals
hold Trump as the Chosen One,
as does he himself!

How did this awful,
fake Christian end up being
their revered darling?

And Trump Says
follow me and I
will lead you to the Promised
Land—they believe him!

But that Promised Land
is for straight, white, middle class
men who feel they're lost.

Low Income Housing
Trump won't let the poor
ruin the 'suburban dreams'
of middle-class snobs.

Day 23 – 31 July

627, 8

8.30 a.m.
Waking up to what?
A world in total turmoil
on the edge of time.

What Next?
In light of numbers
Dan assesses restrictions,
what else can he do?

Stage 4
Stage 4 lockdown is
considered with essential
services only—

supermarkets and
pharmacies, petrol stations,
healthcare—that's all folks!

Togetherness?
The togetherness
we saw in the beginning
is dissipating.

Cracks Emerging
Cracks are emerging
between Fed. and state pollies
tensions are brewing.

Masks Mandated Now
Masks are mandatory
across all jurisdictions
of Victoria.

Interlude—Closing the Gap
Meanwhile another
landmark—an agreement on
Closing the Gap signed.

Milestone Total
Ten thousand cases.
From little things big things grow,
Victoria's surge.

Beginnings
It's hard to believe
it began with one single
person in Wuhan?

'Karen' Speaks
*It's my right as a
living woman to do what-
ever I want to.*

We All Had Plans
A new world order,
we all had plans for the year
before the virus.

Cannot Say BLM
White supremacists
cannot bring themselves to say
that Black Lives Matter.

Mask Burners
Conspiracists burn
masks in an act of dissent,
book burners are born

new pandemic term
is invented to describe
them—*covidiots*.

Sucking the Oxygen
COVID sucks all the
oxygen from everything,
nothing else matters.

Complacency
It's complacency,
young people let down their guard
putting us at risk.

Why?
What draws people to
believe in conspiracies,
hoaxes, schemes and plots?

And what outcome do
they actually want? There's no
logic to their stance

no discernible
or concrete conclusion that
seems to be offered.

Do they want to start
a revolution, a change
of government, bring

down Wall Street, empower
the poor, house the homeless and
kill psychiatry?

Shelter
The COVID tempest.
I need shelter from the storm,
keep me from the rocks.

Zoom!!
A screen-time world now.
Zoom meetings are all the go—
Zoom, Zoom, Zoom, Zoom, Zoom.

Zoom company shares
have skyrocketed on Wall
Street. Wish I'd bought some!

The Curve
Curve is not flattening,
New Zealand-type restrictions
now on the table.

Disproportionate
The pandemic deaths
are disproportionately
black Americans.

God Bless Donald
God bless Donald Trump
for making America
ungreat evermore.

Fiscal Cliff
US in trouble,
economy speeds to cliff,
to fall over edge?

Focus
Trump defiantly
focuses on election,
ignores country's plight.

Day 24 – 1 August

397, 3

Come Home to Roost?
We patted ourselves
on the back during first wave,
have second wave chooks.

Frontline Heroes
Frontline health workers,
the heroes in this fight, are
sacrificial lambs.

From Dan
*Nurses, ambos and
doctors are playing their part.
You need to play yours.*

Warning
Dan is warning that
*community transmission
a growing concern*

and he laments the
confronting aged care outbreaks
and oldies at risk.

When the Music Stopped
March 2020
was the month when music stopped
and lockdown began.

Theatres were emptied
stages a void of silence
and the Arts were dead.

Pandemic Elegy—After Sophie Black
During the first wave
morale-boosting messages
graced our homes and streets,

now rainbows have peeled
off fences along empty
suburban streets, while

the chalk pictures on
our paths have long washed away.
A deep spectral fear

hangs over Melbourne
like a widow's long black veil.
Life is so different,

playgrounds taped over,
the CBD deserted,
skate bowls gravelled up.

First hot spots were named,
then the towers were locked down,
our togetherness

lost, but still there are
men in high-vis vests and hats
building our city.

For what and whom? We
live in a ghost town, zombies
in designer masks,

shrugging off grief by
acknowledging that others
are so much worse off—

the people battling
mental illness, losing homes,
the ones unemployed,

those losing loved ones,
they are among us—neighbours,
friends and work colleagues.

We envy other
states their beaches and cafés
while we're pariahs.

First wave fear is back.
Before an end was in sight,
now there is no end.

Trying to make sense
of an unravelling world
that is downright mad.

COVID Dress Code
Hobo wear, jim-jams,
nothing very flash or smart.
Who is watching us

in our COVID homes?
No one's coming down the drive
to see us dressed down.

Economics
Economics of
pandemic, collateral
damage everywhere.

Where Are They?
One in four people
who have tested positive,
are not in their homes!

Trump's Admiration
Trump's admiration
for foreign dictators is
deeply concerning.

No Surprise
His wish to postpone
the November election
does not surprise us.

Day 25 – 2 August

671, 7

On the Brink
Victorians are
on the brink of hard lockdown—
desperate measures now.

Vic. Mystery Cases
Concerns growing for
mystery cases not yet traced,
where the hell are they?

Behemoth Unleashed
Behemoth virus,
unstoppable juggernaut,
a monster unleashed.

Unsung Heroes
Pathologists sit
in their labs and test up a
storm—unsung heroes.

Sacrifices
With this virus, we're
asked to make sacrifices
for the greater good.

Yet
climate change garners
no effort for greater good,
no moral action.

Post Pandemic
Post pandemic—who
will bear the economic
burden? The young folks?

Collision Course
Civil liberties
and government policies
on collision course.

Environment
The global pause in
human activity has
freed the skies of smog,

the Himalayas
have been seen for the first time,
their peaks in clear sky.

Haemorrhaging Hope
The world crumbles and
each one of us feels the weight,
we're haemorrhaging hope.

1 p.m. – More Restrictions?
Holding our breath, we
are waiting for Dan's update,
more bad news to come?

2.30 p.m.—It Just Got a Whole Lot Worse
State of Disaster
declared by Dan—Stage 4 to
stem the virus flow.

Curfew for Melbourne,
businesses shut, schools to close,
confined to our homes,

must shop and do our
exercise no more than five
kilometres out.

Hundreds of mystery
cases have forced government
to act more broadly.

Week one of six weeks,
we're back at the beginning
of a long, long road.

Six long weeks will be
the toughest of times and the
loneliest of days.

Federal Support?
Federal Cabinet says
they're behind Dan with his tough
new rules. But are they?

What Will 'Karen' Do?
She'll be up in arms
about these tougher measures
claiming human rights.

Vaccine Nationalism
When a vaccine is
found, will self-interest affect
its distribution?

Man-made Pandemic
Virus creates a
man-made pandemic of fear,
mistrust, suspicion.

Lost
Feeling a bit lost
and overwhelmed by despair
that circles my head.

Psychotic Hell
The COVID horror
has escalated into
a psychotic hell.

Hyperbole
Hyperbolic words
to capture the essence and
magnitude of times.

May We Live In
interesting times? May
I live in boring times where
nothing bad happens.

Head in Sand
While Trump puts his head
in the sand, the pandemic
will not go away.

House Divided
Trump's divided house
wages war against itself—
it cannot stand up.

Interlude—My Voices
My voices claimed *they*
were the genesis of the
pandemic! Get real,

talk about having
delusions of grandeur. They're
so full of themselves.

In spite of all this
my sanity is holding
firm through the chaos.

TeleTherapy All the Go
It's a new world now,
therapy on Skype, chatting
to shrinks remotely.

Nattering on the
net doesn't quite cut it
for me but it is

better than nothing.
I would prefer face to face.
Madness can run deep

and from a distance
fool shrinks not to see it and
nip it in the bud.

Berlin
Protests in Berlin
against virus restrictions—
there's world-wide unrest.

State of Disaster

Stage 4 Restrictions

Declared by Premier Daniel Andrews on 2 August

Melbourne's Lifemare

After 25 days of Lockdown 2.0 in Victoria and in spite of the Stage 3 restrictions, the number of new cases, now in the hundreds each day, coupled with a growing number of deaths in aged care facilities, saw a dangerous situation starting to escalate out of control. The State Government acted, and on Sunday 2 August Premier Daniel Andrews declared a *State of Disaster* and Stage 4 restrictions were introduced. Victoria became separated from the rest of Australia and effectively an island. The Stage 4 restrictions were to last a further six weeks. The new, tougher measures would shut down Melbourne's businesses and, with a nightly curfew make the city a virtual ghost town. Things just got a whole lot worse for Melburnians.

Stage 4 Restrictions

From 6 p.m. on Sunday 2 August, if you live in metropolitan Melbourne, Stage 4 restrictions apply. A curfew is in place between the hours of 8 p.m. until 5 a.m. This means you must be at your home during these hours. The only reasons to leave home between 8 p.m. and 5 a.m. will be work, medical care and caregiving. Exemptions include visiting a person with whom you are in an intimate, personal relationship, including outside metropolitan Melbourne.

The four reasons that you can leave home remain, but further limitations are now in place for:

1. Shopping for food or other essential items within 5 kilometres of your home, or at the nearest available supermarket, limited to one person per household, once per day

2. Exercise (applies to outdoor exercise, and with only one other person for one hour only and within 5 kilometres of your home)
3. Permitted work
4. Caregiving, for compassionate reasons or to seek medical treatment also remains a permitted reason to leave home.

As much as you can, you must stay at home. When you leave home, you must use a face covering, unless you have a lawful reason for not doing so.

Gatherings of people: Private: no visitors. Public: up to two people maximum, including a member of your household. People must work from home: Employers must not allow employees to work from workplace if reasonably practicable to work from home.

Schools: Remote learning state-wide, including Year 11 and 12s, except for vulnerable children and children of permitted workers. Specialist schools open for vulnerable children and children of permitted workers (from Wednesday 5 August). Childcare and kinder: closed, except for vulnerable children and children of permitted workers.

Requirement for face coverings, hygiene measures, record keeping, density and physical distancing requirements.

Community sport: closed. Indoor sport and recreation: closed. Outdoor sport: only allowed to exercise with one other person or a member of your household. Recreation: activities such as fishing, golf, boating, tennis, surfing and drive range shooting are not allowed. Outdoor sporting facilities: closed. Swimming pools: closed. Playcentres: closed. Playgrounds: closed. Shopping, retail and personal services: closed, except for click and collect. Restaurants and cafes: take away and delivery only. Pubs, bars, clubs, nightclubs: closed, bottle shop and take away only. Food courts: closed. Beauty and personal care services: closed, apart from hairdressers. Saunas and bathhouses: closed. Auction houses to operate remotely. Real estate auctions and inspections to operate remotely, and inspections by appointment. Markets stalls:

stalls can operate for provision of take away food and drink only. Markets and shopping centres: open, subject to density quotient, but people can only visit for necessary goods and services.

Libraries and community venues: to host an essential public support service or funeral only. Galleries, museums, zoos: closed. Outdoor amusement parks and arcades: closed. Indoor cinemas: closed. Drive-in cinemas: closed. Concert venues, theatres, auditoriums: closed. Arenas and stadiums: closed. Casinos and gaming: closed. Brothels, strip clubs and sex on premise venues: closed. Religious ceremonies and private worship: broadcast only, limit of five people. Weddings: not permitted (from 11.59 p.m. Wednesday 5 August). Funerals: up to ten people, plus those conducting the funeral. Attending a funeral is a permitted reason to leave home and a permitted reason to leave metropolitan Melbourne.

Travel in a vehicle with a person outside your household not permitted, with some exceptions. Travel within Victoria outside metropolitan Melbourne: allowed for work, education (if necessary), and care/compassionate purposes only. Holiday accommodation and camping: closed except for residents, emergency accommodation, or work purposes. You cannot visit second place of residence with limited exceptions (e.g. emergency or maintenance; shared custody; to stay with intimate partner who does not live with you).

Day 1 – 3 August

429 cases, 13 deaths

State of Disaster
hangs over our heads
like something from World War II.
This is serious.

Oh, the Joy
A new day dawned with
Stage 4 restrictions in place.
Oh, what joyful days.

First Day
First day of Stage 4,
this is going to be a
most interesting time.

Six More Weeks
Six more weeks of a
heavy duty lockdown—from
nightmare to lifemare.

Sky Won't Fall In
I'm sure the sun will
keep rising and the sky won't
fall in—well, not yet.

What Fuels Fear?
Pandemic fear—what
fuels it? Inequality
and disparity.

More Powers
Police have more powers to
maintain social control and
keep everyone safe.

Baited Breath
CBD workers
wait with baited breath for Dan's
announcement today.

Travel Bubble Off
Trans-Tasman travel
bubble off the agenda
at least till next year.

New Panic
Shoppers panic. They
are buying meat and veg but
not toilet paper.

Sick City
More pain for Melbourne
already sick with a bout
of anxiety.

On the Beach
Deserted streets like
the set of *On the Beach* haunt
Melbourne's CBD.

Emotions
Emotions range from
fear, anger, quiet despair,
at *shock and awe* rules.

Punch Drunk
The wind knocked out of
us, our confidence shaken,
we're punch-drunk boxers.

Dark Undercurrents
Fractures and fissures
simmering below surface,
dark undercurrents.

Surreal
Why do I feel like
I am in a surrealist
work of zombie art?

This Epoch
This will go down as
our angst-laden epoch, like
no other era.

Those who survive it
will carry the COVID scars
for many years hence.

Going Down Like Flies
Health workers going
down like flies with the virus,
some in ICUs.

Dan's Press Conferences
Daily updates are
our compulsive viewing with
a ghoulish interest.

Other Organs
Coronavirus
attacks more than just the lungs,
other organs too.

Tasmania Border Closed
Tasmania to keep
its border closed to the rest
of the other states.

No Playbook
There is no playbook
about how to manage a
global pandemic.

3.30 p.m. — Dan Announces
a significant
scaling down of businesses,
so tough times ahead.

Shops, cafes, hotels,
pubs, clothing stores, you name it,
it's closed for business,

Long list of closures—
it's business Armageddon.
Who will survive this?

Historic Shutdown
Biggest shut down in
Victoria's history
'unprecedented'.

Interlude—Rescue Packs
Rescue packs sent from
interstate relatives to
brighten our spirits—

chocolates and lollies,
self-care products and funny
novelty items.

Will Not Be Tamed
Sadly, the virus
will not be tamed until a
safe vaccine is found.

Schools
All students to do
remote learning—schools to close,
students in limbo.

No Bloody Sourdough
No talk of bloody
sourdough now or craft or
knitting or felting,

the conversation
has moved to darker places
for these darker times.

Curfew Unthinkable
The idea of a
night curfew on Melbourne was
just unthinkable.

No Stage 5
There is no Stage 5,
Stage 4 has to work—there is
nowhere else to go.

Holes and Gaps
The holes and gaps in
our preparedness for the
pandemic exposed.

Meanwhile
Florida hit by
a tropical storm—what else
can bloody go wrong?

Haiku Hope
Creativity
a panacea for the
plague times upon us.

Day 2 – 4 August

439, 11

New Penalties
On deadly day, tough
new virus penalties are
announced by Andrews.

COVID Winter Blues
While Melbourne shivers,
we quiver in the bitter
COVID winter blues.

Mental Health of Nation
Mental health at risk—
anxiety, depression,
suicide lurking.

Interlude—Infodemic
An infodemic.
Super-spreader celebs push
false information.

Disinformation
Disinformation
is spread to destabilise
some democracies.

Dark New Chapter
We're entering a
dark new chapter of unknown
plots and characters.

Let's Pause
Let's pause for a while
and take stock of these troubled
times that assail us.

Shattered Dreams
How many people's
dreams have been shattered by the
coronavirus?

Interlude—Unconditional Love
Small things bolster hope,
like our cats and dog who love
unconditionally.

No Choice
The new normal we
have to get used to—we know
we have no choice here.

Once in a Generation
Yep, a once in a
generation life event—
what to make of it?

Pandemic Payment
Paid pandemic leave
to aid significant pain
the workers will bear.

Above the Law
'Sovereign citizens'
with their wild theories drawn from
social media

baiting police at
checkpoints, refusing to give
names and addresses.

They're not abiding
by the law, putting us all
at substantial risk.

250,000
people will be stood
down as thousands of shops and
businesses shut up

not to mention the
factories that will close their doors
because of Stage 4

they are joining the
thousands of others who have
already lost work.

Meanwhile
500,000
are already working from home,
the new working life.

Shelves Stripped
Food chain is secure,
yet panic buying erupts
and shelves stripped of meat.

Necessary Step
Harsher lockdown a
necessary step—this is
war with a virus.

Be Positive
The words are pouring
out, imploring us to hope
and be positive.

Interlude—Uluru Closed
Uluru closed, as
traditional owners fear
visitors coming

on flights that pass through
Brisbane—a COVID hotspot—
will spread the virus.

Time Passes
Day by day, week by
week, month by month, time passes
ever so slowly.

This is Serious
Trump's soapie would be
a hoot if it were not so
bloody serious.

Interlude—Cold, Wintry Day
It's a cold, wintry
day—rain, hail and snow—gloomy
weather, gloomy days.

Day 3 – 5 August

725, 15

Darkest Day
The numbers are in—
records tumble yet again
poor Victoria.

New Name
A new name for our
ailing State: *Sictoria*—
says it all really.

Survival
Some businesses who
got through the first wave may not
survive the second.

A Cliff
Businesses feel that
they are being walked over
a deep, yawning cliff.

Last day
It's Melbourne's last day
of normal trade before shops
have to close their doors.

Humbling
As much as we strive,
the virus is humbling us—
we are powerless.

The Path Ahead
A long grinding task,
the path to normality
is long and winding.

Sheer Numbers
The sheer numbers of
cases in Vic. make tracing
unachievable.

Curfew Ghost Roads
Vision from cameras
on main Melbourne roads show them
as empty ghost roads

a grateful premier
says *thanks* to Melburnians
for keeping curfew.

The World is Watching
The world is watching
Melbourne's Stage 4 lockdown to
see what they can learn.

Permits
Permits needed now
to show why you are not at
home during curfew.

Border Closure Again
Queensland closes its
borders to ACT and
also New South Wales.

Two-Week Quarantine
People now entering
Qld from New South Wales must
two-week quarantine.

Dan's Looking Tired
Dan's looking tired,
his eyes ringed with black, his face
drawn and deeply grim.

For weeks and weeks, he's
had to deliver the tough,
sad, daily updates.

Questions Asked
Questions over the
resourcing of the Vic. Health
Department, are asked.

Interlude—Winter Blast
Rain, hail, sun, cold, snow,
cold, rain, hail, snow, cold, sun, hail,
rain, cold, hail, sun, snow.

'Wonder' Drug
Sales of 'wonder' drug
hydroxychloroquine spike
as Trump extols it.

We're Doing Great
We're doing great. Trump
insists that the virus is
under good control.

Trump is out of his
depth, and does not seem to care
about his people.

Old People Dying
Half of COVID deaths
in USA are older
people in aged care.

Day 4 – 6 August

471, 8

Dan's Update
Cases still too high
and more deaths to report on—
Melbourne limping on.

A Vaccine?
Russia to start a
mass vaccination programme—
a vaccine? Stay tuned.

Virgin Airline
Virgin announces
three thousand redundancies,
airline in distress.

Dark Alliance
Anti-vaxxers and
5G COVID protestors
join dark alliance.

Bearing the Brunt
Aged care is bearing
the brunt of the infections
and, sadly, the deaths.

From ScoMo
From ScoMo to us:
we have to keep our heads up
and *let's get through this.*

New South Wales
Gladys appeals to
State's youth to modify their
risky behaviour.

Knife's Edge
New South Wales is on
a knife's edge halfway through a
most critical time.

Over 700,000 Global Deaths
As the death toll climbs,
the world is gripped by fear for
our unknown future.

ADF Personnel
Personnel from the
ADF enlisted in
Vic. for doorknocking.

**The Singer Sewing Machine
is Running Hot**
Home-made mask maker,
our Singer is running hot,
mask production-line.

Mystery Cases
continue to be
a significant problem—
they cannot be traced.

Holding Our Breath
We hold our breath while
asking: when will the numbers
finally come down?

Inquiry
Inquiry into
the hotel quarantine mess
underway in Vic.

Trump Interview Goes Viral
Trump's chat with journo
Swan reveals his ignorance,
and it goes viral.

It is what it is,
says Trump about the death toll
in America.

Can Trump spin his way
out of this dilemma, yes,
it is what it is

he has succeeded,
spinning his way out of this
with his bald face lies.

Trump Versus Fauci
Trump versus Fauci,
tensions between them arise,
Trump will not listen

Fauci warns of *long
road ahead*, Trump says virus
will *go away soon.*

Day 5 – 7 August

450, 11

Steadying Ship
Steadying of ship?
We are hopeful—wishing for
sunny days ahead.

Essential Service
Liquor shops deemed to
be essential services—
elixir of life?

Fault Lines
Fault lines are exposed,
there are more racial attacks
against some Asians.

New Enthusiasm
Purchases of bikes
shows new enthusiasm
for joy of riding.

Two Australias
Pandemic sees us
living in two Australias—
Melbourne and the rest

of Australia whose
lives are now almost normal,
at least socially.

The Country is Behind Us
The whole country is
hoping that Stage 4 in Vic.
contains the virus.

Interlude—Super Spreaders
Mercenaries who are
fighting in Syria are
spreading the virus.

Internet Workout
The internet has
been getting a workout with
all the online stuff.

What's Next?
We have evolved past
panic buying toilet rolls.
I wonder what's next?

Special Consideration
will be given to
students doing VCE
and their ATAR scores.

Circus Success
Friends say how they are
grateful for the footy—the
circus is working.

Ghost Town
Nearby Yarra Glen
is a ghost town—all it needs
are the tumbleweeds.

Doomsday Dread
State of Disaster,
language has a serious
tone of doomsday dread.

Legal Action
Families are looking
at legal action against
some retirement homes.

The Upwards Curve
The curve is trending
upwards. How to flatten it?
With a sledgehammer.

Over One Thousand
Concerns as over
one thousand health workers test
virus positive,

mostly nurses, aged
care and ancillary staff
rather than doctors.

Loony Tunes
Unrest grows, people
frustrated and attracted
to loony ideas.

Failure?
If Stage 4 fails the
future becomes too awful
to even think of.

Survival Strategy
COVID Cuisine—a
menu of delicious food,
on a whiteboard which

we viewed every day
to whet our appetites for
our nightly pleasure.

Carping
Lib. Opposition
are carping at Dan from the
sideline. They'd do what?

Land Army
Crops may go unpicked
with fruit falling to the ground—
no workers to pick.

Let's mobilise a
Land Army like in World War
Two when young women

signed up to work on
farms—ploughing, stacking hay or
other jobs needed.

A nation in need
and people pulled together.
Can we do that now?

From across the Ditch
100 days free
of community spread. We
can learn from Kiwis.

Day 6 – 8 August

466, 12

COVID Dog
The COVID dog is
howling in the night seeking
to inhabit us.

Point Scoring
Politicians point
score off the virus's pain,
that's very poor form.

Meaningless
We are more and more
living in a meaningless,
bizarre universe.

Prof. Sutton Says
Chief Health Officer
says the restrictions will help
drive down the numbers.

Haikus for Dan
The wolves are circling
you Dan, baying for your blood
watching and waiting

for the slip-up as
you lead us through this crisis
without a playbook.

Day after day you
stand before us bravely, a
grey North Face jacket

hugging your shoulders,
holding up your tense body,
grim face with grim news.

You never flinch or
shy away from the bleak task.
I hope you're honest.

The COVID blues have
hit us hard, our hope dwindling
each difficult day.

You could never have
imagined, on taking power,
such a pandemic.

Such a challenge to
your leadership, and failure
a hair's breadth away.

You stand tall and strong
yet you look weary while you're
holding hope for us,

but you steer this ship
of fools to safer waters
while the wolves circle.

Reserve Bank Warns
Reserve Bank warns that
the nation is in for more
economic pain.

200 People Fined
Vic. police have been
fining people for breaking
COVID-19 rules.

Exponential Increase
We have averted
an exponential increase
in COVID cases.

Right Wingers
Right wingers who hold
contrarian views about
letting old die are

playing bingo at
the Styx, the numbers called are
lucky ones condemned.

Day 7 – 9 August

394, 17

8 a.m.
A quiet morning,
in passive holding pattern
awaiting the day.

Some Stabilisation
Numbers suggest a
stabilisation of new
cases in districts.

17 Deaths
Death toll hits a new
record, sadly, they're mainly
senior citizens.

New Trend
Disturbing new trend
has doctors worried—younger
folks getting virus

as second person
under 30 has died from
contracting virus.

Long Term Impacts
Concerns about the
long term impacts of virus
in younger people

even if you are
young, recovery may take
many, many months.

Christmas 2020
Premier can't give an
assurance that Christmas will
be a normal one.

Favipiravir
Scramble to find drugs
to treat virus—hopes now for
existing flu drug.

The Strain Is Showing
Leaders are under
enormous pressure and the
strain is now showing.

Toughest Week
One of the toughest
weeks yet, for Dan, with daily
cases hitting peak.

Jenny Mikakos Tweeted
I've worked every day
to keep everyone safe. If
it wasn't enough

I'm deeply sorry,
but *contagious viruses*
are unforgiving.

Increased Demands
Increasing demands
on our acute mental health
services, concern

self-harm has increased,
need for support has never
been greater for some.

Support for Carers
Support for carers
with increased demands on them,
new package announced.

What Would They Say?
What would women who
wear a hjjab say about
our face coverings?

On the Streets
Police and army
walk the streets to keep the peace.
A new world order?

Day 8 – 10 August

322, 19

National Toll
The deadliest news,
national toll 300,
steep rise in nine days.

Mike Baird Says
in defence of Dan:
*It's not the time to second
guess or finger point.*

Matthew Guy Says
coward colleagues are
defending Dan Andrews—he
is fed up with them.

Aged Care
We pay strangers a
pittance to look after our
old folks in care homes

because we are not
prepared or able to care
for them ourselves and

now they are dying
in alarming numbers in
virus riddled homes.

Any wonder there
is a Royal Commission
into the sector.

Aged Care Royal Commission Reveals
Fed. government had
no plans for COVID outbreak
in their nursing homes.

What Will Change Post Pandemic?
Not politics where
hyper-partisanism
will sadly snap back.

Pollies will still be
saying the unsayable
on breakfast telly

and getting lots of
media attention and
notoriety.

Politics won't change
and politicians will still
act very badly.

Warning
While the case numbers
fall, Dan warns us that it is
just *one day's data*.

Patience and Kindness
We need to offer
each other, in these sad times,
patience and kindness.

COVID Distractions
TV shows offer
a much-needed distraction—
banal, benign, crime,

*Miss Marple, Poirot,
Diagnosis Murder* and
Midsomer Murders.

There is no damage
psychologically if one
watches these shows, and

they always get their
man, and restore the proper
ethical order.

We're all streaming shows—
it is the pandemic vibe,
seeking comfort in

episodes of past
favourites, living in their
world to escape ours.

It's Time for Soul Searching
What does our work mean?
How are our relationships?
These questions and more,

a time to ponder
the meaning of life and our
place in this odd world.

Believing Myths
Young people and men
are more likely to believe
myths about virus.

Holding Our Breath
Trump or Biden? The
COVID US election—
the world holds its breath.

Has the Tap Turned Off?
Haikus were pouring
out of my soul like water—
has the tap turned off?

No, they come like gifts
from the poetry Goddess,
my lifesaver Muse.

Day 9 – 11 August

331, 19

Shifting Sands
Media have moved
from the 'impact and response'
phase to the 'blame' game.

May explain why the
political unity,
the 'togetherness'

rhetoric, is now
starting to fray a little
around the edges.

Has Dan been able
to read this shift in reproach?
Is he losing ground?

Finally, Some Good News
The first signs that Vic.
is finally getting on
top of second wave,

our sacrifices
are paying off—infection
rates trending downwards

but more heartbreak lies
ahead for families, as more
deaths are expected.

NSW Anxiety
COVID cases hit
a four-month high—worry now
for potential spread.

COVID Mortgage Stress
As each day passes
young families are on the cusp
of losing their homes.

Middle Game of COVID
A greater use of
isolation would help us
through the 'middle game'.

Trump's Dream
*Do you know, it's my
dream to have my face on Mount
Rushmore.* Yep, dream on.

Day 10 – 12 August

410, 21

For Victorians
every day now is
our darkest day, with record
numbers of those dead.

New Zealand Lockdown Again
We were looking at
New Zealand's success, cases
eradicated,

100 days free
of virus—now fresh outbreak
poses a real threat,

four new cases found
in a family in Auckland
have caused the lockdown,

residents await
the contact tracing results
to see what happens.

Jacinda Ardern
is calling for calm in light
of new virus risk,

a need to *go hard
and early* to avoid the
risk of wide outbreak.

Back to the future
for New Zealand as they now
grapple with virus.

Russia Approves
the world's first vaccine
hailed by Moscow as proof of
scientific clout

and the resolve of
Russia to win the global
race for a vaccine.

Are they putting their
prestige before sound science
and people's safety?

Puffed up Putin is
boastful of the achievement,
some are sceptical.

20 Million
World cases surging,
six months for 10 million and
six weeks to 20.

US, India
and Brazil account for half
of those large numbers.

NSW
Tip of the iceberg,
growing school clusters sparks fear
of virus outbreak

and patient zero
remains a mystery at one
independent school

residents urged to
wear a mask when venturing
outside—*just do it*.

US Elections—Kamala Harris
Biden chooses a
Jamaican-Indian-born
woman running-mate.

Day 11 – 13 August

278, 8

Some Hope
An optimistic
fall in case numbers gives us
cause to hold some hope.

Expect More Deaths
Even as cases
fall, more deaths are expected,
but things looking up.

Paradox
A funny thing—the
COVID days drag, yet five months
have flown by quickly!

Avoid the Fate of Victoria
New South Wales must learn
and avoid the fate facing
Dan's Victoria.

Hotel Quarantine Inquiry
War of words between
Fed. and state governments—was
ADF offered?

Spat Intensifies
Spat, between the Feds
and state over quarantine
mess, intensifies.

Government Messages About
coronavirus
are 'nonsensical' as they're
badly translated

errors found in Fed.
and state messages aimed at
other languages.

French Champagne Crisis
Bubbly down gurgler,
sales worse than Great Depression,
no toasting good health,

cork put on weddings,
parties, dining out—bottles
languish in cellars.

But Alcohol Consumption Up
People are drinking
more alcohol to rid them
of the COVID blues—

beer, spirits, wine—
people are on the sauce and
drowning their sorrows.

House Prices
House prices are tipped
to fall as we brace for rise
in unemployment.

Empathy Works
Jacinda, the most
popular NZ PM
in 50 years. Wow,

politics of warmth
and kindness, a breath of fresh
political air.

Royal Commission—
Blistering Revelations
Aged care is still not
prepared for COVID—Federal
government hammered.

Virus Climbs in Regional Areas
Virus is spreading,
shutdown is a *'day-by-day*
proposition', Dan.

Overdue Reckoning
Biden ticket is
long overdue reckoning
with their racism.

Day 12 – 14 August

372, 14

Up and Down We Go
Coronacoaster
continues with up and down
numbers for each day,

yesterday's figures
were hopefully down, today
they are up again.

Bravo Teachers
Teachers have tough gig.
I am in awe of them, with
their onerous tasks.

Students
Difficult times for
VCE students in their
most pivotal year.

Terrorism Lull
World's attention is
focussed on virus—global
terrorism lull.

Front and Centre
Pandemic is still
in the forefront of our minds,
nothing else matters.

Youngest to Die
Man in twenties dies,
Australia's youngest victim
of the pandemic.

Hospital Infections
Royal Melbourne forced to
shut wards and move patients to
other hospitals

virus infections
have spread to staff and patients—
fears for their safety.

Fed. Liberals' COVID Solution
How to rebuild the
economy?—build a gas
pipeline across Oz.

Theories
Economists are
debating economic
policy world-wide.

What will post-COVID
economies look like when
pandemic eases?

Money
Money transactions
discouraged—EFTPOS and cards
the desired way,

money is seen as
a germ carrier, filthy
lucre that infects.

Makeup
Masks hiding faces
have caused lipstick sales to drop,
but eye makeup soars.

Complacent
Were we complacent
in January when the
pandemic started?

And did we miss an
opportunity to be
much better prepared?

Rush and Hurry Lifestyle
Will we stop the rushed
and hurried lifestyle we are
accustomed to now

and ditch the endless
lists we ticked off every day?
No more headless chooks!

Day 13 – 15 August

303, 4

Money
Fifty-dollar notes,
for now, are being hoarded
by worried people.

Jenny Mikakos Feels the Heat
I've been unlucky
to land in a once-in-a-
hundred-year event.

Sacrificed
Have the elderly
been sacrificed? Hospital
beds reserved for young.

Corporate Dress
Has the pandemic
killed off corporate dress—the suit
and power dressing?

Folk Festivals Cancelled
Iconic Woodford
and Port Fairy sadly not
going ahead—blow.

Ardern Juggernaut
Jacinda, from glass
cliff to global acclaim, she's
making big, big waves.

Buck-Passing Pollies
It's been exhausting
watching our leaders buck-pass
and shifting the blame,

the virus has no
interest in which leader can
stonewall the longest.

Psychology
Most of us are on
an emotional roller-
coaster, ups and downs,

mood carousel in
freefall, oscillating from
upbeat to downbeat.

Interlude—Footy
Demons crush the Pies,
surprising win against a
good team—miracle.

From one Collingwood
supporter: *Bloody COVID
and now this*. Go Dees!

**Republicans Flummoxed—
Racist Birtherism**
Kamala Harris
choice by Biden has thrown cat
among the pigeons.

Trump calls her *nasty*,
condescending, he even
tries to say she's *mad*.

Trump promotes idea:
Harris ineligible
for the high office
of Vice-President
claiming she's not a natural
born citizen. But

Trump can't help himself,
goes for the lowest common
denominator,

his negative tone
fails to lift America
from dysphoria.

Day 14 – 16 August

279, 16

Right Direction
Heading in the right
direction, but we *are in
an endurance race,*

hope is that we are
stemming the second wave and
strategy's working?

Signs
Victoria shows
signs the worst of the horror
second wave has passed.

Encouraging Signs in Melbourne but
more progress needed
before Stage 4 restrictions/
lockdown can be eased.

Border Closure
Separated by
pandemic, families cannot
bring loved ones back home.

New Zealand Investigates
whether its COVID
infections could be linked to
Melbourne storage place.

Counting My Blessings
COVID blues impinge,
but there are worse off people.
I count my blessings.

Blame the Elderly
Narrative seems to
blame the elderly as the
cause of pandemic.

Cosmetic Surgery Spike
from people who view
themselves on Zoom meetings and
don't like what they see.

State Opposition Leader
Scathing assessment
of O'Brien—*The Assistant
Librarian*. True.

Pollies' Thoughts and Prayers
Thoughts and prayers go out
to all those who have lost their
loved ones in aged care.

Extension
Andrews extends the
State of Emergency to
September 13.

Move Over Ivanka
Time to move over
Ivanka, Kamala is
smart *and* stylish.

Day 15 – 17 August

282, 25

Counting the Dead
Toll hits tragic high,
deadliest pandemic day
but infections fall.

Trend
Sub-300 day,
Victoria appears to
have surpassed the peak.

Taking Toll
COVID taking toll,
two premiers under pressure,
yep, Dan and Gladys.

Pandemic Effect
Isolation for
autistic community,
strain on services.

High Hopes
There are high hopes for
a vaccine, clinical trials
are now underway.

False Claims
People cited false
psych. issues to get out of
their quarantine rooms

saying that they were
suicidal and at risk,
and it worked for them.

Hotel Inquiry
Damning evidence
about the training of guards,
muddled and confused.

Pessimism Trap
We cannot allow
ourselves to buy into the
pessimism trap.

Day 16 – 18 August

222, 17

That Important Curve
The curve is starting
to flatten—finally some
gain for the raw pain.

Virus Christmas Miracle
A miracle if
three states open their borders
for Christmas this year.

99 Per Cent
of Victoria's
second wave can be traced to
two Melbourne hotels.

Ruby Princess
*Inexcusable,
inexplicable*—verdict
from boat inquiry.

Apology
Gladys gives a most
heartfelt apology to
Ruby Princess trades.

Lives on Hold
Our lives are on hold—
whatever gives us meaning
is no longer there.

Dwindling
Haiku storm abates,
words are becalmed, ideas flat
and poems dwindle.

Time Markers
Six months gone and I
can't account for the days and
months of this vexed time.

Bucolic Paradise
I look out of the
window and see bush and birds.
No pandemic there.

Day 17 – 19 August

216, 12

PM Deflects
PM deflects Fed's
responsibility for
the aged care crisis

that has rocked aged care
in Victoria, with most
deaths in that sector.

Vaccine Deal
Day of hope for us,
Australia signs a deal with
AstraZeneca

for vaccine that is
being developed by the
Oxford Uni folks.

It's contingent on
it proving successful in
all the human trials.

But Prof. Sutton says:
*we shouldn't hang our hat on
one vaccine* only.

Mandatory Vaccine
PM says vaccine
would be mandatory for all.
And anti-vaxxers?

Anti-Vaxxers' Fury
Anti-vaxxers are
up in arms: *you can't make us
have this vaccine.* Hmm ...

Margaret Atwoodesque
We have put our faith
in vaccine science, who knows
what will happen down

the track with vaccines?
I can feel an Atwood time
coming on, when two

years after we are
vaccinated, we'll all drop
dead curiously

from some mutation
that turns the vaccines rogue and
they become killers.

Grumpy Old Men Leaders
Angry old men are
ruling and ruining the
world—all narcissists.

Trump, Putin, Jinping,
foster personality
cults around themselves.

We need a vaccine
for grumpy old men leaders
who cling to the past

because if we are
going to create a new
post-pandemic world

we don't want leaders
who are crass, self-serving fools,
crowding the world stage.

Trump Election Warning
Trump poses idea
if he loses election
then it must be rigged.

Day 18 – 20 August

240, 13

COVID Tests Down in Victoria
Number of tests done
have fallen—why are people
not having the test?

Victoria's Restrictions
won't be eased quickly,
no blueprint for what to do,
numbers still too high.

Sweden
Sweden opted for
herd immunity—now they
are paying the price,

Europe
Europe is grappling
with a second wave outbreak—
all eyes are on them.

Open Again
Skate parks and playgrounds
are open again—people
are very happy.

Qantas's Profit Plunges
Qantas's profit
plunges 91 per cent,
turbulence ahead.

Pressure
Pressure from Qantas
to open state borders as
airline crashes out.

It's Working!
Melbourne lockdown is
working but is affecting
people's mental health.

Frankston Hospital Cluster
Frankston Hospital
cluster is causing concern—
virus ramping up.

Australia Post
Australia Post is
booming—parcels delivered
by pony express.

Pat Cash Conspiracy Theory
Virus created
by Fauci, in league with his
rich, powerful friends.

Cash copped a broadside
on social media for
this idiocy.

Interlude—Germany Concerns
Average age of those
infected in Germany
is now much younger.

Day 19 – 21 August

179, 9

Some Light?
Is there light at the
end of the COVID tunnel?
Things are more hopeful

for the first time in
weeks new cases have fallen
below 200.

Haiku Central
Haikus inhabit
my mind and my study is
now *haiku central*.

Flip Flop
PM flip flops on
mandatory vaccine and will
'encourage' uptake.

Come Down Hard
Calls from medicos
to come down hard on those who
refuse the vaccine.

Small Suspicions
become a major
paranoia when stories
become toxic tales.

Tough Gig
Tough gig being in
Opposition not to sound
like bloody whingers.

Hatred of the One Per Cent
Loathing of the one
per cent heightens when they start
to feather their nests.

Fake Politics
Have we just been through
a decade where politics
became fakery?

And our faith in it
has dwindled so far that we
hate politicians?

US Elections 2020
Biden: *united*
we can and will overcome
this awful darkness.

He delivers the
most inspiring speech of his
political life

as he accepts the
nomination for office
of the President.

As an Empire Falls
Is American
exceptionalism no
longer a hard truth?

We watch the US
with keen interest, unable
to avert our gaze.

Like all empires, its
time has come when its power
no longer holds sway.

Day 20 – 22 August

182, 13

Welcome News
Two days in a row
under 200—welcome
news for plague city.

A Conspiracy Theory
Big Pharma, in league
with medicos, created
virus to make dosh.

I Wonder?
What is it like to
live with strange conspiracies
controlling your mind,

not trusting pollies,
journalists, scientists and
scholars—paranoid

and living with fringe
ideas on the fringe of the
ordinary world?

$165 a Pop!
London Fashion House
launches very expensive
collection of masks.

1918 Spanish Flu
WHO hopes pandemic
could be a bit shorter than
1918 flu

but with the world more
connected, the virus has
better chance to spread.

Once and for All
Local researchers
test hydroxychloroquine's
efficacious worth

because it has been
politicised. We need to
settle the science.

Generation Divide
Younger Australians
are worse off than their parents
were at the same age

they face things that their
predecessors didn't—wage
stagnation, net debt,

underemployment,
resources going to the
old and climate change.

The American Psyche
Michelle Obama
says depression has struck, *she's
not her usual self.*

Americans are
depressed, anxious, heaviness
saturates their hearts,

summer in US
feels like the end of time, it's
a broken country.

Will We Survive?
Can the world and the
US survive another
four years of Donald?

'Sleepy Joe' Awakes
'Sleepy Joe' awakes
from his slumber and fires huge
shot in election,

*we're in a battle
for the soul of the nation,*
Biden lambasts Trump.

News Flash
China is handling
pandemic better than the
USA—fake news?

Day 21 – 23 August

208, 17

Milestones
As we reach milestones
they are grim reminders of
new reality.

TV Show Shutdown
The Masked Singer stars
and crew, forced to isolate,
seven cases found.

Data Pause
Dan has not released
virus modelling data—the
maths of life and death.

NT: First COVID Election
Labor loses seats
but may still form government.
Gunner positive.

COVID Condolences
Everyday Dan has
to send his *condolences
to those affected.*

Blursdays
Today is blursday,
tomorrow is blursday, then
blursday, blursday, blurrrrr …

Today is
the 23rd of
something. Yep, the months just morph
into nothingness,

*like sands through the hour
glass,* so are the drifting days
of our COVID lives.

Pandemic Word
The most used word in
these pandemic times is *grim*—
an apt description.

Thank God
Thank God for the gift
of creativity—a
way to process things.

Global Deaths Top 800,000
The misery of
death continues, with rising
toll reaching new heights.

Reading Trump
Democrats failed to
read Trump four years ago, will
they do it again?

Day 22 – 24 August

116, 15

Plunging Figures
Finally, some hope,
case numbers plunge—signs that we
are moving through this.

Deaths in Australia—517
Milestone: 500
deaths passed and rising—they are
sobering numbers.

Halfway Mark
We're halfway through Stage
4 restrictions, and things look
more optimistic.

Dull Moment?
There's never a dull
moment with virus, things are
constantly moving.

Recycling Problems
Single use plastic,
PPE equipment and
disposable masks

ending up in land
fill, lying in gutters, a
recycling headache.

Parliament Zoom
Screens are erected,
parliament to be Zoomed to
help pollies attend.

Restrictions in Vic.
make attending Canberra
much too difficult.

State of Emergency
Dan wants to extend
State of Emergency for
another 12 months.

Big call for Andrews,
the Opposition see it
as a power grab.

Grieving
There is grieving to
do for things that once defined
our identities.

Trump's Niece Dumps
Trump's niece dumps on him—
he's *cruel*, *a phoney* and he's
a liar. Well, well.

Day 23 – 25 August

148, 8

Some Relief
Steady as we go,
numbers are falling, trending
in right direction.

Re-infected
For first time a man
has been infected by two
strains of the virus

new case questions the
efficacy of vaccines—
yep, sneaky virus.

State of Emergency Extension
Legislation would
ensure rules for public health
could still be enforced.

Dan Needs to Explain
how extending the
State of Emergency won't
impact our freedoms.

The Paranoia of Some
Dan's proposal makes
conspiracy theorists wild
with paranoia.

Ethical Quandary
Church leaders' concerns—
some vaccines use cells from an
aborted foetus,

so, Catholics are urged
to boycott those vaccines that
are unethical.

Christmas
Festive season to
look a bit different this year—
purse strings are tightened.

In Control?
States appear to be
in control of the virus
battle—that's good news.

Dr Coatsworth Says
we all have duty
to thank Victorians for
what they are doing

for the nation, what
is going on down there is
for our benefit.

Borders Easing with Victoria
New South Wales and South
Australia are easing their
border restrictions

after pressure from
border communities who
have suffered big time.

Interlude—USA: BLDM
Another unarmed
black man shot by the police—
Black Lives *Don't* Matter

as George Floyd's spectre
haunts America with his
last words: *I can't breathe.*

Day 24 – 26 August

149, 24

Hard to Deal With
The daily deaths that
occur from the virus are
so hard to deal with.

Squabbling Continues
Feds and Vics squabble
over aged care deaths—this blame
game is not helpful.

Better than Expected
Australian vaccine
proves better than expected,
results shared with world.

State of Emergency Extension
does not mean Stage 4
restrictions will continue
for another year.

Television
Local stations are
struggling—advertising has
dried up, viewers flee.

Scary Thought: A Trump Dynasty
Trump wants to create
a dynasty to rival
the Kennedys, and

Trump Jr is the
front runner, but Ivanka
is waiting in wings

Republican Convention
Trump children are full
of hate speech—Republicans
are fuelling this storm,

they cry *four more years!*
Trump quips *Twelve!* He's serious,
dictator yearnings.

Day 25 – 27 August

113, 23

113 New Cases
The lowest number
since July—a good trend to
have at last for Vic.

Sad Truth
The sad truth is that
virus failures have wiped out
the elderly folks.

Warning
Premier has a stern
warning of a third wave for
we Victorians.

Frankston Hospital Cluster
sees 600 health
workers in quarantine—that's
a lot of people.

NSW
Clusters are starting
to emerge at various
locations in State.

Day 26 – 28th August

113, 12

Double Digits Soon?
Are we heading to
rare double-digit cases
in the next few days?

Another Big Day
Yawn, get up, wash hair,
Nutri-grain, walk, paper, read,
haikus, Dan, big day.

Habituated
I wonder if I
am habituated to
the COVID lifestyle?

New Relevance
Drive-ins make a come
back—old fashioned idea
has new relevance.

Cowardly Colbeck
Aged care minster
walks out of senate Chamber
after questions asked.

Backdown
Dan backs down on *State
of Emergency* Bill—he
can't get the numbers.

He is still talking
to crossbench to pass Bill for
extension powers.

Twelve months seems a long
time, not sure why he didn't
want to try for six.

Lifeline
Lifeline calls through the
roof—community's mental
health falling apart.

Schoolies Week
Gold Coast schoolies week
has been cancelled by Queensland
government this year.

Nonsense
Conspiracists are
full of bat-shit-craziness,
so says the police.

USA—Law and Order
US is convulsed
by violence, Trump runs on law
and order ticket.

No Class
A Trump dynasty?
Nah, they don't have the class of
the Kennedy clan.

Poisoned Chalice
If Biden wins the
election, is he getting
a poisoned chalice?

Day 27 – 29 August

94, 18

Finally
Finally, we are
back to double digits—step
in right direction.

But 18 Deaths
People tragically
are still dying—sobering
stats with which we live.

Bomb-Throwing
State Opposition's
bomb-throwing is not helping
us deal with virus.

In Melbourne
we are staring at the
the walls of our apartments—
virus prisoners.

Three Pandemics
New South Wales, Queensland,
Victoria—three states with
different pandemics.

Nature Comes Back
While we have focused
on COVID, nature has been
clawing its way back

from bushfire and drought—
rivers are full, soils are wet
and leaves have regrown.

Spring
Warmer sunny days
offset COVID, but alas
bushfire season looms.

COVID Pastimes
Board games, Lego and
jigsaw puzzles all the rage,
COVID amusements.

USA—Reverend Al Sharpton Said
you might have killed the
dreamer but you can't kill the
dream—truth crushed shall rise.

Trump's Nomination
Lies, more lies, and now
revisionist history marks
Trump's nomination.

Republicans in
alternative universe
where Americans

are not living through
the horrors of COVID and
thousands have not died.

180,000 Dead
Has Trump noticed how
many of his people have
died? Empathy? None.

American Exceptionalism
We are drawn to the
US with a curious
fascination. Why?

Something about its
greatness holds us captive, as
we witness its fall.

USA Back to Sanity
If Biden wins, can
he drag America back
to some sanity?

Ivanka for President
Trump wants Ivanka
as first elected female
US President.

Day 28 – 30 August

114, 11

Whoops
Whoops, here we go, up
again, coronacoaster
fluctuations, whoops.

Epidemiologist Urges
us not to become
complacent about social
distancing measures.

COVID Family Violence
Financial stress and
unemployment are causing
more family violence,

women can break the
curfew if they need to leave
a violent partner.

MP Deal for Dan
Fiona Patten
may give support for six months'
powers extension.

Coronavirus Sceptics
Thousands march across
UK, France and Germany
against restrictions,

imperialist
flags waving, questioning the
truth of the virus

and not wearing masks,
supporting Trump and Putin,
while infections rise.

Slogan
*Staying apart keeps
us together*—a slogan
to rally the troops.

From Dan to Michael O'Brien
Ok Michael, here's
the data and info, now
it's over to you.

Day 29 – 31 August

73, 41

Mixed News
The good news is that
new cases have plummeted—
lowest since July.

The bad news is that
41 people have died—
melancholy tale.

The Greater Good
Most Victorians
seem OK with restrictions—
can see greater good.

Pandemic Recession Is
unduly hurting
Sydney and Melbourne, data
from ABS shows.

Ramping up Pressure
Fed. Libs are ramping
up pressure on Dan, saying
he has no roadmap.

Frydenberg leads the
charge against Dan flying the
Conservatives' flag.

Are Fed. Libs trying
to deflect attention from
their huge aged-care mess?

I loathe this crass fall
into party politics—
it fosters hatred.

5.55 p.m.
Dan will reveal how
our lives will change from the strict
shutdown next Sunday.

He will unveil his
plans for the State post Stage 4
but can't rule out things.

It's Come to This
It's a bit sad when
the highlight of the week is
a cold Diet Coke.

25 Million Global Cases
and deaths are rising,
nearly 900,000—
disturbing figures.

Morbid Fascination
We all seem to have
a morbid fascination
with Donald Trump. Why?

Racism Overcurrent
Trump's appeal to white
middle class—racism is
the *over*current.

Long Winter Gone
It's been a long, hard,
winter of plague and despair,
what will Springtime bring?

Day 30 – 1 September

70, 5

Great Stats
Great stats today with
low cases and low deaths—so
there is some relief.

Legislation
Dan to introduce
extension Bill into the
Upper House today.

At Last
After much grief and
heartache, the aged-care crisis
now slowly eases.

The Plan
Two roadmaps planned—1/
metropolitan Melbourne,
2/ regional Vic.

Cluster Alarm
New South Wales has an
alarming cluster building—
train and bus alert.

India
has fastest growing
rate of infection, yet they're
easing restrictions.

WHO warns this is a
recipe for disaster
and stupidity.

ScoMo's Push
PM wants borders
as normal as possible
in time for Christmas.

Preferential Treatment
Is PM going
too easy on SA and
Tassie while he's hard

on Labor states? It
seems party politics
are getting in way.

We're Tired
We just want it to
be over now, as COVID
weariness sets in.

Day 31 – 2 September

90, 6

The Numbers are Slightly Up
As we near the end
of Stage 4, the trend is now
showing improvement.

Emergency Bill Passes
Marathon sitting
sees Dan's extension Bill pass,
now to Lower House.

Toxic Tony Abbott Says
*fear of falling sick
stops us from being fully
alive … people should*

*get on with their lives
even in the presence of
death,* and *media*

*have indulged in a
virus hysteria.* He's
a climate sceptic

COVID denier
happy to let the old die.
GLAD he's NOT PM!

Blame
Some Vics feel they are
being blamed for pandemic,
they're calling Lifeline,

exhausted health care
workers are among callers,
burnt out and depressed.

Not Supported
Some Victorians
feel lack of support from the
rest of the country.

Young People Are
missing the fun and
laughter and playtime their lives
would normally have

increases in self—
harm, risk of suicide and
troubling behaviour

they're bearing the brunt
of the lockdown at school, at
uni and at work.

The Mental Health Toll
As we endure the
prolonged lockdown, mental health
workers see impact

heightened fear with the
financial stress and loss of
control, all factors.

Not What it Used to Be
Reality is
not what it used to be, the
nightmare continues.

Economic Devastation
Worst growth figures since
records started—contraction
of seven per cent

our first recession
since 1991—it
is a long road back.

In spite of these dire
numbers, ScoMo will make cuts
to welfare payments.

Spotlight
Royal Commission
and pandemic have put the
spotlight on aged care.

AFL Grand Final
Footy final moves
to the Gabba—a move forced
by the pandemic.

Pandemic Passivity
I trust that I am
going to be kept safe but
how do I know this?

Day 32 – 3 September

113, 15

Oh Dear
Our double digit
stats have reverted to old
triple figure ways.

Regional Victoria
Low regional stats
may allow their restrictions
to ease more quickly.

The Protracted Path
Path out of COVID
recession is protracted,
weighed down by concerns

about health, winding
back of welfare payments with
current restrictions.

Social Distancing
People becoming
slack with social distancing,
vigilance required.

Strutting
Abbott struts the world
stage with self-importance and
clear stupidity.

Professor Brendan Crabb Says
Vic. and New South Wales
should have elimination
race to rid virus.

Dan's Roadmap
*The roadmap will be
guided by the science and
the data, not dates.*

Rumours
circulate that Stage
4 restrictions are going
to be extended.

State government says
the leaked draft is out of date—
we await the truth

but there may be months
of some type of restrictions
ahead of us still.

The COVID Unemployment Industry
is raking in the
money they have made on the
backs of unemployed.

Social Inequality
The pandemic has
exacerbated social
inequality.

Feds are looking at
tax cuts for the rich as their
recovery plan.

Wellness Podcast
State Library offers
bibliotherapy, the
healing strength of books

as a wellness tool
for Victorians in these
most difficult times.

Uni Student COVID Stress
40 per cent of
uni students contemplate
taking their own life

as stresses mount, with
remote learning, no campus
life and no support.

Liberties
Poor optics—police
handcuff a pregnant woman
and charge her for the

crime of inciting
dissent in a Facebook post.
We do not know the

history behind this
story or if she set up
a Facebook scene, but

these heavy handed
tactics have become, for some,
a crucial issue.

We have to ask: what
are we prepared to lose in
the grim COVID fight?

The tension between
COVID rules and freedom is
starting to ignite.

No Psychological Help
Vulnerable patients
are unable to access
psychologists' help,

waiting times are long,
psychologists' books are full,
session numbers capped.

Day 33 – 4 September

81, 59

Deadliest Day
Return to welcome
downward trend but we record
our deadliest day.

Flicking the Switch
PM anxious to
flick switch to optimism
as country flounders.

Online Retail Therapy
We're buying toys, clothes,
entertainment, eating in—
all online shopping.

Propping Up Spending
JobKeeper has put
a floor under consumer
spending—when it goes?

Welfare Timebomb
Ticking timebomb for
those on welfare—wind backs mean
poverty beckons.

The Lonely Pandemic
When the loneliness
epidemic collided
with the pandemic

an experiment
in mass isolation had
suddenly begun.

Fragmented people
are feeling disconnected.
COVID loneliness

is driving them to
helplines and psych wards—many
feel voiceless and lost

and now the shift from
the collectivist to the
personal has made

a society
of lonely people who feel
so invisible.

Yep, loneliness is
trending in the zeitgeist, in
this, the new century

of solitudes, in
which we crave connection while
we are kept apart.

Pandemic Farewell
Farewell dad, I am
so sorry that I had to
witness your last breath

on video call,
laments a daughter who could
not be with her dad.

Election Politics
Premiers facing an
election, play hardball on
their border closures.

Opening State Borders
PM unable
to get consensus among
Territory and

State leaders, angry
ScoMo scolds their border plans,
he wants a roll back.

Virus Free for Weeks
Western Australia
is without community
transmission for weeks.

Interlude — British Press Label Abbott
homophobic, he's
a sexist-misogynist-
climate denier.

They question if he
is the right person for the
plum UK trade job.

The S Word
Trump threatens US
with socialism if they
elect Joe Biden.

Do They Know?
Do Americans
know what socialism is?
McCarthy lingers.

Day 34 – 5 September

76, 11

By December
Aim to open the
borders by December is
supported by states

except the wild West—
they're still holding out and will
keep their border closed.

Disunity
The unity of
the National Cabinet
is somewhat fractured.

Make Australia Whole Again
ScoMo wants to make
Australia whole again post
pandemic dramas.

People's
fear of becoming
infected is the roadblock
to recovery.

NSW Schools
Ban on school formals
to be lifted—kids can have
their end of year bash.

Virus Update
Race for vaccine hots
up and WHO anticipates
rollout in next year.

Meanwhile Russia is
bullish about its vaccine
coded Sputnik-V.

WHO is stressing the
importance of testing the
drugs' efficacy

before rolling them
out—but will national pride
produce useless jabs?

The Summer the Music Died
The helpless music
industry is on the verge
of COVID collapse.

Not just musos but
sound and lighting experts may
leave the industry.

Insolvencies
Banks say there will be
insolvencies when support
is withdrawn, as some

businesses are close
to bankruptcy and many
face going under.

Reservoir of Patience
Sitting in psych. wards
for months at Larundel gave
me the tools I need

to survive lockdown—
a reservoir of patience
to just sit and wait.

Anti-Lockdown Protests
Chants of *Dictator
Dan* at Shrine of Remembrance
protest this morning,

and anti-lockdown
protests across the country
show deep displeasure

and scepticism,
*there is no epidemic
just State tyranny.*

Are they singing from
the US playbook with all
its conspiracies?

Tensions are rising
between civil liberty
groups and the police.

The unrest highlights
a divide between COVID
belief and distrust.

Is it politics,
or denial and ignorance,
that drives these beliefs?

The things that bind us
are being tested by these
fractured, wayward times.

Teflon Man
Trump presides over
massive COVID death toll yet
nothing seems to stick.

Lawless US Streets
Visibility
of armed groups on the streets is
a worrying trend.

Lawlessness, unrest,
violence, vigilantes,
are urged on by Trump.

Day 35 – 6 September

63, 5

The Mood Has Shifted
Mood has shifted from
goodwill to blame and protest,
anger spills over

people are anxious,
worrying about money,
their jobs, the future.

Looking Back
When we look back on
this time, will the things that drew
us together or

pulled us apart be
remembered—what will it tell
us about ourselves?

Empty CBD?
Will people working
from home ever go back to
city office blocks?

250 Days of COVID-19
From patient zero
in Wuhan, the contagion
spread like wildfire.

26 million
infected, tens of thousands
dead, and the world flipped.

Schools, unis, shut doors,
remote learning plans devised,
kids without iPads

or computers are
shut out from learning, while some
will never return.

Hugs, kisses, handshakes
banned, video calls, emails
replace face to face.

The internet is
our lifeline *and* breeding ground
for conspiracies.

Lockdown has become
a civil-liberties stoush
between State and mobs.

Unemployment is
massive and now we have a
a global downturn.

Business has ground to
a halt, the arts demolished,
concert halls empty,

women, the young and
low-income workers are hit
the hardest, meanwhile

travel ceases, planes
are grounded, borders are closed,
families kept apart.

The world is reeling,
we lurch through each day in this
cruel COVID lifemare

numbering the days
that drag on, with no end in
sight, no light, no hope.

12 noon—Dan's Roadmap to Recovery: Metropolitan Melbourne
Stage 4 restrictions
to last two more weeks with some
tweaking of the rules.

Three month roadmap for
state heading to a Christmas
that's close to normal.

The curfew will be
eased, social bubbles for those
who live alone, and

we can exercise
for longer, opening up
will be done in steps

progressing as we
hit clear numbers of cases
on rolling average.

*We can't open up
too fast* for fear of a third
wave—we're aiming for

a COVID Normal,
with no new cases for at
least 28 days.

*We can't run out of
lockdown, we have to take safe,
steady steps*, says Dan.

Regional Victoria
They begin Stage 2
earlier than Melbourne—with
gradual easing,

each step depends on
the data—if the number
of cases decrease.

What Will People Say?
How will this roadmap
be viewed by Victorians?
With hope or despair?

Caution
Dan's cautious plan is
irking PM and Josh who
carp from the sidelines.

What would they do in
Dan's position? Open up
and let us all die?

Day 36 – 7 September

41, 9

10 Week Low
Latest data shows
a marked improvement of new
cases—ten-week low.

Health vs Commerce
Dan's roadmap ignites
debate between health workers
and business people.

Once again, our health
is pitted against commerce,
there's no easy way.

Business Despair
Business reaction
is despair, predicting dire
costs to small traders.

Federation
The Federation
of states and Feds is tested
with states holding out.

Driving Seat
Premiers are in the
driving seat and will not be
rushed into action.

ScoMo is annoyed
and wants swifter opening
of economy.

Vaccine Pipeline
Some vaccines are still
in pipeline but hopes are high
of a quick rollout.

Interlude—Morning Walk
The colonies of
orchids are stunning to see.
Spring looks promising.

Day 37 – 8 September

55, 8

Politics
What does ScoMo want?
To throw caution to the wind?
It's all politics.

Health Over Popularity
Dan says he's putting
people's lives over his own
popularity.

Leadership
Never before has
leadership mattered so much
as we all struggle.

Only Grief
If I were Dan, I'd
kiss the job goodbye—there is
only grief for him.

Stages of Grief
Anger fuels many,
while others say the roadmap
can't be right, as the

modelling must be wrong.
Some ask: *why can't we have a
different arrangement*

*for the regions that
are less affected?* While those
with depression need

help from mental health
practitioners. Yet others
accept their fate and

knuckle down, hoping
that they will soon be able
to forget this year.

Business exhibits
bold optimism that, if
we open up, there

will be no adverse
effects and no real prospect
of lockdown again.

Pressure from PM
ScoMo's pressure—he's
trying to shame Dan into
relaxing the rules.

Ugly politics
is playing into people's
insecurities.

You'll Be Shot in the Philippines
Duterte warns that
people who flout the curfew
could be shot on sight.

Election Game Changer
Trump expects he will
announce a vaccine before
US election.

He's banking on this
to win— putting all his eggs
in the jab basket.

India: 90,000 Cases in a Day
Now second behind
US for numbers—it's not
going well for them.

Day 38 – 9 September

76, 11

76, 11
Stubborn figures keep
us on virus alert—we
cannot ignore it.

At Risk
Scientists find that
men and the elderly have
weaker immune risks.

Picking up the Slack?
Are non-parents now
taking up the slack at work
for workers with kids?

Suspension of Drug Trial
AstraZeneca
suspends trial after adverse
reaction to drug.

A Link
Overweight people
become more severely ill
from COVID-19.

COVID-19 Conspiracies
Fragmentation of
the narrative into weird
conspiracies shows

inability
for us to have basis for
sensible debate.

Is the Anti-Christ
about to inhabit us,
or is it a push

by the powerful
elite to control us? Who
or what inflames this

disaffection in
the hearts and minds of people
fearing the unknown?

Vaccine Politics
Will governments put
pressure on researchers to
fast track a vaccine?

If Frustration and Anger Were
a vaccine against
this virus, we'd be in a
better position.

Apollo Bay
Viral fragments have
been detected in the waste
water of the town.

Sleepless in Victoria
Dan's looking tired,
drawn and very stressed—is he
getting enough sleep?

Celebrity Favours?
Are celebrities
getting special exemptions
to cross the borders?

Day 39 – 10 September

51, 7

These Strange Times
Feels like I'm in a
George Orwell novel in a
dystopic nightmare.

QAnon
Isolation has
driven people to the web
for information

the weirdness of their
extreme beliefs cannot be
understated, yet

QAnon rides the
wave of right-wing madness, of
paranoia and

frustration with the
COVID pandemic, and those
who are gullible

and vulnerable are
ripe to be influenced by
misinformation.

It is the wild west
internet where all facts are
irrelevant. It's

US-Trump-centric,
a collective delusion,
a collapse of truth

where people cannot
deal with the things beyond their
imagination.

And who the hell's Q
hiding anonymously
behind a keyboard?

In this Conspiracy
Satan-worshiping
cabals of paedophiles rule
the world, they control

politicians, the
media, and Hollywood,
were it not for Trump

who's come to save us.
Their language is religious,
apocalyptic

and cultish, and it
attracts odd bods and those who
research the dark web.

COVID loneliness
and estrangement create a
perfect storm, where the

forces for Trump will
forge *The Great Awakening*
and mend this bad world.

Trump has become a
cult figure for his groupies—
this is dangerous.

The Numbers
aren't a simple truth,
epidemiology
is political,

who has the best way
of testing for the virus
is debatable.

COVID Mental Health
Unstoppable trend
has emerged—we are *talking*
about mental health!

My Poor Diary
is lonely and now
has Attention Deficit
Disorder. It is

in poor mental health.
Can pathologizing it
help it to get well?

The Libs Versus Dan
The gloves are off and
normal hostilities have
resumed between the

Libs and Dan, who is
their first target, their *bête noir*.
They're out to get him

by whipping up a
Dictator Dan frenzy to
destabilise him.

Flashpoint
A border battle
ignites over a funeral.
Palaszczuk says that

Scott Morrison is
bullying her. Politics
of division rules.

Day 40 – 11 September

43, 9

43, 9
State is trying to
meet the threshold so we can
reopen for trade.

Dan's Pledge
*A COVID-normal
Christmas without restrictive,
tough virus measures.*

Interlude—Sydney Olympics
It is 20 short
years since Cathy lit the flame
and sport ruled the world.

9/11
19 years on from
that fateful day when terror
came into our lives.

Preferential Treatment
It's problematic,
AFL, celebrities
get special treatment,

the optics aren't good,
red carpet, luxury digs
rolled out for these folks

but for those who can't
get in to attend funerals
of deceased parents

it seems harsh and cruel.
Are premiers holding too fast
to their strict borders?

No Show at Hospitals
Sharp drop in people
going to emergency
departments for help.

Christmas Window
Myer's most famous
Christmas window display has
been cancelled this year.

Country Victoria
is poised to take a
step or two out of virus
restrictions in days.

Toxic Leaders in Time of COVID-19
Xi, Bolsonaro,
Putin, Johnson, Duterte
Trump, Kim Jong-un are

the leaders we have
who are either murderers,
buffoons or liars.

Will the world collapse
into a chaos and ruin
under their egos?

Trump Antics
Sound angry, say you're
angry, act angry, pretend
angry—fakery.

Day 41 – 12 September

37, 6

Some Light at Last
We were losing hope
that things would improve, but now
there's some light at last.

Stockholm Syndrome
Have we formed a strange
bond with Dan who has us in
this COVID lockdown?

Mortgage Holidays End
as people begin
to repay bank loans after
six-month deferral.

Curfew Questions
Dan's curfew causes
questions about its legal
status to be asked.

More Questions
Contact tracing in
Vic. comes under scrutiny—
a hotchpotch muddle?

Set to Return
Hairdressing and pet
grooming is set to return,
but masks must be worn.

Nobel Prize and Trump
Trump's nomination
for the Nobel Prize has fed
his foolish hubris,

already he is
insufferable about it,
his ego puffed up.

Day 42 – 13 September

41, 7

State of Emergency and Disaster
Four-week extension
giving police powers to
enforce directions.

Metro Hope
Metro Melbourne is
offered some hope by progress
in regional Vic.

Regional Coffee
Coffee or a meal
in cafés may soon be on
the cards for regions.

Calls to Ease Restrictions
Melbourne to remain
in Stage 4 amid growing
calls to ease the rules.

My Mad Comrades Say
welcome to our world
of forced isolation, and
depression, madness

and anxiety,
no friends, no work—we can tell
you all about it.

Thank God
My aversion to
hugging is vindicated—
now there's no pressure.

Vaccine Trial Resumed
Oxford vaccine trial
resumes after pause was caused
by a woman who

developed severe
neurological symptoms-
safety must come first.

15 Federal Mental Health Clinics
will open to the
public, with teams of mental
health professionals

to provide on-site
support, and to connect folks
with other mental

health services in
their region—integration
is key to success.

COVID-19 is a Genetically Engineered
virus by the world
banks to kill off all weaker
human beings, says

Tony Pecora,
a one-time candidate for
Clive Palmer's party

who's organised the
protests at the Shrine, holding
placards demanding

churches be opened,
liberty and *Sack Andrews.*
Wackadoodledee?

Interlude—US Record Firestorms
California and
Oregon are ravaged by
record firestorms,

mass fatalities
expected, thousands of homes
destroyed in days, and

eerie scorched ruins
of small towns made rubble by
the blaze, smoulder. The

US, and at home,
we are at the mercy of
climate change weather.

Americans
are entering the
eighth month of their crisis with
little choice but to

grapple with death and
habituate the horror
they are living with.

Yet, the death toll has
not put a stop to the states
opening up or

swayed conversation,
steering it towards action.
They are in limbo.

France: 10,000 Cases
France records massive
10,000 cases in one
day amidst unrest.

If
If you can make one
person believe in Virgin
Births, Resurrections,

Holy Trinities,
then a conspiracy is
not impossible.

Day 43 – 14 September

35, 7

Some Good News
for businesses, with
Dan announcing a package
of three billion dollars.

to help small business
ride out the virus lockdown
and get back on feet.

Back Off
AMA tells the
critics to back off Queensland
over border spat.

Queensland's
Chief Health Officer
has received death threats, as things
become more toxic.

Arrests in Melbourne
There were dozens of
arrests of protestors on
eve of lockdown cuts.

A Different Summer
Boxing Day Test and
Australian Open are in
some lingering doubt.

If He Loses
If Trump loses the
election, will he call out
the Guard and stay put?

Day 44 – 15 September

42, 0

At Last
At last, a day with
no deaths— heartening news for all
Melburnians—yay.

COVID Reflections
Now that we have had
more time to sit and think, what
have we discovered?

We've had to address
how we treat the elderly,
do we respect them?

Regional Opening
Regional Vic. is
set to reopen with some
restrictions to ease.

The Politics of a Funeral
Family unhappy
with PM's attempt to make
political gain

from the family's grief.
It's tawdry point scoring and
unedifying.

Rebuilding after COVID
Manufacturing
is set to be rebuilt to
make stuff locally.

Interlude—Cathy's Race
Cathy united
Australia in 49
brief seconds but then

we undid all the
good work—sadly racism
never goes away.

Personal Attacks
Attacks on Dan get
personal, people stooping
to low, mean measures.

Divided State
Ring of steel divides
Melbourne from regional Vic.,
strict roadblocks in place,

people discouraged
from leaving Melbourne—police
patrol the roads out.

The Optics
Police can't afford
to act improperly, they
will lose their support,

stomping on someone's
head, shooting the mentally
ill, are bad optics.

Day 45 – 17 September

28, 8

Plunge
Infections plunge to
a three-month low, welcome news
for our tired ears.

Border Easing
New South Wales eases
restrictions on Vic. border—
relief for many.

Winter Influenza
Northern hemisphere
virus spread worry, as the
winter season looms.

Milestone
India passes
five million cases—second
country to do so.

My Diary Not Only Has
ADD, it has
Abandonment Syndrome and
needs a talking cure.

COVID Friend Bubble
One friend only can
be selected to enter
a bubble, but who?

Friends are feeling the
rejection of not being,
yes, the Chosen One!

Dan Fights Back
Cheap politics is
no vaccine against virus
says Dan, fighting back.

Surprise
Unemployment rate
has fallen, a surprise for
most economists.

Age Care Nomenclature
They used to be called
'nursing homes' now they are called
aged-care homes because

there's not a nurse in
sight—staff are not trained for the
work they have to do.

Dear Santa
I would like to play
hockey, play music with my
bands, see friends, live in

a post-COVID world,
see Dan re-elected, Trump
dumped and yes, world peace.

Day 46 – 18 September

45, 5

Cases Jump
Jump in cases with
concerns for a cluster in
Hallam and Casey,

five households flout the
rules causing virus breakout
endangering us.

Irony
Can you believe it,
bankruptcy practitioners
are on JobKeeper?

Jobs Rebound
Job rebound surprise
is positive sign for the
economy. Wow.

Policy Genius
JobKeeper was a
stroke of genius that has
kept people in work.

Why?
Why is government
running unis into the
ground? Crude politics?

The mood across the
uni sector grows bleaker,
more job cuts proposed.

Shared Experience
It's loneliness that
is shared by many people
in this pandemic.

Petering Out
I thought my haikus
were petering out, but there's
loads to write about.

Glass Half-Full
My half-full COVID
glass only sees doom and gloom
and more doom and gloom.

Europe Alarm
A virus surge in
Europe alarms WHO—cases
exceed the first peak.

24,000 Australians are
stranded in foreign
lands and want to come home but
can't get onto flights

which are over-priced
and beyond the means of most
ordinary folks.

Limits
States agree to a
staggered rise in their hotel
quarantine limits.

Day 47 – 19 September

21, 7

Tracking
We are tracking for
restrictions to be eased—it's
a long time coming.

Government Failings?
Pressure builds on Dan
from hotel inquiry—too
many failings bared.

Mutual Obligation
Punitive system
to return for job seekers—
humiliation.

Another Milestone
30 million world-
wide cases with the US
still the front runner.

Here's Another One
Ablett Senior says:
the Illuminati and
Freemasons for years

have worked to found a
new world order to enthrone
Lucifer. And the

virus was made and
released by them, to disguise
their globalist aims

of a cashless world
that will lead to the Mark of
the Beast as foretold.

Vaccines will kill us
and so, reduce our numbers.
The pandemic is

proof the end times are
near and the Second Coming
is soon to happen.

Christ, as a King, will
take over and crush evil,
His throne will be in

Jerusalem—*the
rapture of the church is close,
it is imminent.*

I stifle my laughs
at this mumbo-jumbo but
people believe it.

Interlude—Trump offered Assange a
pardon in exchange
for details of who hacked the
Democrats' emails

which damaged Clinton's
tilt for the Presidency,
London Court has heard.

Election Scam?
Trump calls election
a scam if Biden wins, but
what if Trump wins? Scam?

Why?
Why are so many
Americans dying in
this *wealthy* country?

The not-so-hidden
inequalities are now
exposed by virus.

Blueprint for Vaccine Released by
drug companies to
counter Trump's claim of *soon-to-
be-released* vaccine.

Death Traps
US, Brazil and
India are death traps for
millions of people.

Britain's Second Wave
unstoppable, says
Boris, who's considering
whether to lockdown.

Day 48 – 20 September

14, 5

Tracking
Vic. tracking towards
lockdown lift, as infections
hit a three-month low.

At Last, PTL
Praise the Lord, maybe
Dan's lockdown is working as
the cases decrease.

The Protestors
So, are they freedom-
fighters or a selfish few
endangering us?

Perhaps activists
should look overseas to see
what is happening.

China Vaccine
Thousands of Chinese
have been given a vaccine—
rigorous trials? No.

Golden Age
A golden age of
conspiracy theories. Why?
Plague anxiety?

30 per cent of
Americans believe in
a conspiracy

about the virus
which is weaponised by some
politicians who

knowingly will spread
misinformation to aid
their own election.

It is madness on
steroids from so-called sane folks,
it's far-fetched, absurd.

Their Bollywood lights,
camera, action, all singing,
dancing loony tunes

makes us Schizos look
like the sanest people out.
Why aren't *they* in a

psychiatric ward,
medicated, restrained and
in the hands of shrinks

to deal with their mad,
delusional, confused thoughts,
instead of poor us?

Fear-mongering from
news outlets like Sky News and
the *Herald-Sun*, or

the net they surf with
fervour, feeds them with blatant,
rank, fabrications

that unhinges their
perplexed minds while they teeter.
It is just bonkers.

The world needs to be
brought back to sanity, so
forget the fluoride,

spike the water with
Zyprexa, Lithium and
mood-lifter Prozac!

And when COVID is
over, will all the crazies
in the psych. wards be

reassessed, because
who's mad and who's sane is not
that clear anymore!

Day 49 – 21 September

11, 2

Dare to Hope
Melburnians are
buoyed by figures that give them
reason for new hope.

Praise our Stoicism
Vics need to be praised
for their stoicism in
their fight with virus.

On Faster Track
We are on track to
hit COVID target faster
than first expected.

Complacency
With case numbers on
the decline there is a fear
of complacency.

How Safe?
How will we go when
it subsides—will we feel safe
when around people?

No Support
International
students are going through hell
with no real supports.

Kids and Mental Health
A surge in mental
health aid for kids—many are
struggling with remote

learning and the hard
lockdown, their lives are on hold
while they battle on.

Calls are being made
to reopen schools as kids
need their school buddies.

You're Not the Voice
Protestors highjack
Farnham's song *You're the Voice* for
rally—John's not pleased.

Public Transport
has never run so
smoothly—no passengers bring
punctual services.

Six Months On
It began with a
festive flavour as people
settled into their

COVID projects, but
things turned when the second wave
hit and suddenly

six months on and we
are in Stage 4 lockdown in
Melbourne. It's been a

long time since we left
our homes, saw friends, played sport or
did normal things that

gave us meaning and
purpose—hope fell away and
we despaired for life.

We are worn down in
our prison homes and only
have 'COVID normal'

to look forward to.
Meanwhile springtime brings its bees,
and flowers—and hope.

Another Depressing US Milestone
200,000
dead—a stern reminder of
how deadly it is.

They're on track to reach
400,000 deaths—when
will Donald listen?

Pandemic Politics
Cascades of falsehoods
ushered in by pandemic.
Apprehension feeds

left nihilism,
far right millenarism,
both disenchanted

with democracy,
while the virus has opened
the political

divide and exposed
the paranoia and the
fantasies in us.

Solidarity's
absence leaves us atomised
and prey to leaders'

nefarious plans,
while sober conservatives
find conspiracy

theories and contempt
for liberal democracy.
History lurches from

an ill-defined state
of stasis into chaos,
twilight closes in.

Day 50 – 22 September

28, 3

Yo-Yo
Yo-Yo numbers are
frustrating but we must look
at the big picture.

Spooks and Phantoms
My spooks and phantoms
came to torment me in the
unforgiving night,

lying in my fright,
fending them off with my thoughts,
clasping sanity.

Roaring Trade
Shrinks are doing a
roaring trade—we're all depressed,
anxious and insane!

The Risk
As things open up,
will we want to put ourselves
at risk of virus?

Restrictions Pressure
Dan: *I'm not looking
to impress people, it's a
matter of science.*

Friendships that Matter
COVID limbo has
sorted fair weather friends from
those that are sincere.

Not all friendships are
created equal—'heart friends'
trump 'alliance friends.'

Day 51 – 23 September

15, 5

Targets Smashed
Melbourne eyes further
freedoms as it smashes Stage
4 virus targets,

some of the strictest
measures may be wound back as
cases pass milestone.

Alarm
Researchers' alarm
about neurological
symptoms—loss of smell

may link the virus
to onset of Parkinson's
disease in some folks.

More Easing
Queensland, New South Wales
and SA are to ease their
border restrictions.

Queensland Anger
Withdrawal of the
border control ADF
by PM seen as

political point
scoring by Queensland who are
angry with PM.

Women's Mental Health
Women three times more
likely to suffer during
COVID pandemic.

Vic. Hotel Inquiry
No one seems to know
who made decision to use
private companies.

Omnibus Bill Questioned
Judges, barristers
question excessive powers
of omnibus bill

an enforcement team
untrained, unprofessional,
may breach human rights.

La La Land Trump
*It affects almost
nobody, it's amazing,*
says La La Land Trump,

trivialising
the pandemic's effect as
huge death toll is reached.

Snake Oil
Modern-day snake oil
sellers and conspiracies,
fool presidents and

world leaders, MPs
and birdbrained believers, to
put faith in fake cures.

Meanwhile
the COVID Guru
Dr Norman Swan imparts
his COVID wisdom

on the ABC
each morning— what a relief,
no pseudo-babble.

Europe Second Wave
UK, Spain caught up
in deadly second wave, so
hard lockdowns brought back.

Day 52 – 24 September

12, 2

Words
*Our thoughts and prayers go
out to families who have lost
loved ones*, goes the spiel.

We Wait
We wait with bated
breath for Dan's weekend address,
will some freedom come?

12 Noon—Dan Cautions Us
Dan dashes hopes of
early return to freedom,
instead, steady steps.

*We will not just throw
open the doors ... the roadmap
does not speak to that.*

Universities
The guts have been ripped
out of unis—they are a
shell of what they were,

and morale at them
is at its lowest ebb with
thousands of jobs gone.

Quicksand
We walk on mental
quicksand—do we sink or swim
in the COVID mire?

Vaccine Race
may entrench divide
between poor and rich nations
who may hoard vaccines.

Small Business Lifeline
Small businesses who
are struggling thrown lifeline with
bankruptcy reforms.

Travel Bans
Stranded Aussies feel
dumped, cheated on, abandoned
and a hopelessness

while stuck far away
from their homes. They want more help
from the government.

Rejoice
Dancing at weddings,
school sport, back on cards in New
South Wales—welcome news.

Pacifying the Mob
Footy circus seems
to have pacified the mob,
though their perks have irked.

Crims on JobKeeper
Break-ins are down and
there's less crime—criminals must
be on JobKeeper!

Trump Refuses to Commit to
peaceful handover
if he loses election—
the man has no shame.

Day 53 – 25 September

14,8

Financial Reckoning
Jobless on edge of
financial abyss—payments
from JobSeeker slashed.

More Contagious
*Virus becoming
more contagious but not more
deadly,* says scientist.

Family Violence
Violence in homes spikes
during lockdown, highest rates
in the state's history.

Mikakos Support
Nurses' union backs
under-fire minister
Jenny Mikakos.

COVID Brain
Drifting off? You can't
focus? No motivation?
Yep, that's *COVID brain*.

Facing the Music
Dan to face music
at hotel inquiry—what
will he have to say?

A Drop in Numbers
Number of virus
patients in Vic. hospitals
below 500.

6.24 p.m.—Hotel Inquiry
*I don't know … we were
buying time to prepare a
health system,* said Dan

as they expected
things to unfold as they had
in other countries.

Jenny Mikakos
is the *minster who was
responsible*. So

how will Dan be judged?
The knives are out, the wolves
are baying for blood

lack of answers means
media are going to
have a big field day

Tourism Welcomes
Border easing is
welcomed by the tourism
trade which was hit hard.

COVID Music
Forming our local
trio has been the best thing
to come from COVID.

The three of us lost
in the nourishing music
of Mozart, Haydn,

Dvorak and more.
Classical tunes that soothe the
soul. Two violins and

a cello playing
their own part to make a whole,
our music floating

in and about the
Chrissy Hills while the virus
rages elsewhere. We

hold this music gift
close to our hearts and know that
this is a privilege.

Day 54 – 26 September

12, 1

We Await
We are all waiting
for Dan's address tomorrow—
eager for the news.

Sacrificial Lamb?
Mikakos is the
first head to roll in wake of
hotel inquiry.

And did Dan throw her
under a bus? Possibly.
Ugly politics.

She resigned, sending
Dan a text message—bad blood
between him and her.

She is probably
relieved and saying: Thank God,
I am out of here.

As much as I hate
pollies, I don't envy them
their demanding jobs.

Yes Minister
Now for the fallout,
the new Minister for Health
is Martin Foley.

Bad Optics
Forgetfulness or
no knowledge of are very
bad optics for Dan.

This World
We lament a world
ruled by demagogues, petty
tyrants and class clowns.

We're on our knees with
a rampant killer virus,
fear stalks everyone,

we worry that dark,
digital forces are out
to terminate us.

What legacy are
we leaving our grandchildren?
And yet, 80 years

ago Hitler ran
amok, jack-booting his way
across Europe, things

looked dire and the world
was surely at its end time.
But the world survived.

Grand Final?
Today would have been
the AFL Grand Final—
MCG empty.

Toxic Race
Vaccine race getting
toxic, no guarantee of
ethical sharing.

Day 55 – 27 September

16, 2

12.30 p.m.—All Important Update
Curfew lifted, some
folks back to work, among
some of the changes.

I hoped for bigger
easing, to be able to
play with my trio.

Not yet, as Dan takes
a conservative line to
avoid third lockdown.

We are looking to
mid-October for bigger
restrictions easing.

Three more weeks of hard
rules. I'll have to draw on my
patience reservoir.

Vaccine Wars
The PM urges
countries to share their vaccines.
Are you listening Trump?

'Save Our Stages'
Vast majority
of live venues will close for
ever without help.

Bracing for Poverty
JobSeekers brace for
poverty as the PM
slashes supplement.

Mikakos Responds
*I'm deeply sorry
for the situation that
Victorians find*

*themselves in. In good
conscience, I do not believe
that my actions led*

to them. Tough times for
disappointed Mikakos.
My integrity,

she says, *has sought to
be undermined.* By whom? Dan?
Watch this deadly space.

3 p.m.—She's Left the Building
Mikakos resigns
and is leaving politics,
she's left the building

and she's probably
burnt out, exhausted and has
had jack of it all.

Conspiritualists
A strange meeting of
the wellness industry and
conspiracists. Yes,

wellness warriors
unite with the alt-right mob
QAnon. How did

love and light go down
this dark rabbit-hole? We fear
uncertainty so

'elites' of science,
politics, Hollywood and
business, become the

target for people
who are terrified, who seek
their truth from sources

in cyberspace or
Facebook, most of it unchecked
information which

they call *research*. Where
are the facts? We struggle to
decipher bullshit.

Conspiritualists
are among us—friends, family—
how to approach them?

US Supreme Court
Spat over Ginsburg's
replacement—her untimely
death creates problems.

Couldn't she have hung
on until after the race?
Huge liberal hole left

which Trump is rushing
to fill with conservative
Judge Amy Barrett.

Trump sets the tone for
a conservative Supreme
Court now for decades.

Interlude—Vatican Chicaneries
Cardinal is caught
up in real estate scandal—
blessed are the poor.

Day 56 – 28 September

5, 3

Finally
Case numbers fall to
single digits—positive
signs going forward.

Be Vigilant
Dan urges us to
not let our guard down, as the
virus can get loose.

Tsunami
Fiscal tsunami
is coming, people will be
drowning in their debt.

Impending Budget
There are calls to boost
social housing, JobSeeker
benefits, rather

than bringing forward
income tax cuts for the rich says
top economists.

Trump and Taxes
Trump paid little tax,
creative accounting saves
him millions of bucks.

Hypocrite
What is worse than a
liar? A liar who is
a double-dealer.

Fakest News
The real fake news is
the fake-pretender-phoney
that Donald Trump is.

Strange Bedfellows
Judge Coney Barrett—
moral, conservative and
of the Catholic faith—

stands next to Trump—the
pussy grabbing, morally
bankrupt, corrupt fraud.

How can she stand in
the same room as him? Has her
ambition trumped her?

Day 57 – 29 September

10, 7

Health Minister Greg Hunt
tells Dan to open
up Melbourne faster—*they can
take safe steps forward.*

Aiming For
We are aiming for
COVID normal, whatever
that actually means.

Evictions
Moratorium
on rental evictions soon
to end in Queensland.

Gold Standard Politics
ScoMo keeps telling
us that New South Wales is the
Gold Standard State as

opposed to the plague
State of Victoria—no
politics seen here?

WHO Announcement
Poorer countries to
get access to rapid tests
for COVID-19.

Another COVID Milestone
World reaches milestone,
one million deaths from COVID
and the toll rises.

Day 58 – 30 September

13, 4

On Right Track Still
14 day rolling
infection average is still
falling, thank the Gods.

Edging Towards
The death toll edges
towards another milestone,
800 deaths loom.

Case Free
Queensland enjoys yet
another day of zero
cases—lucky them!

Inquiry Blame
Three public servants
blamed for not bringing issues
to the minister.

Power
Have our governments
become way too powerful
in these COVID times?

Have executive
powers been probed well enough
by the parliament?

Bombshell
The report into
aged care due to be handed
to the government.

Flaws in the aged care
system exposed, showing the
damning evidence.

Elderly deaths could
have been avoided with fast
action, report shows.

Interlude—Helen Reddy Dead
The voice of the sound
track to my younger student,
feminist years—dead.

The Bunnings Sausage Sizzle
New South Wales and the
ACT set to see some
sizzles return, Yay!

Unpresidential Debate
A car crash that you
couldn't look away from, poor
old America.

Who would bother to
vote in such a broken place,
does civil war loom?

Day 59 – 1 October

15, 2

Well, We're There
800 deaths now
in Victoria—a bleak
marker for the State.

Economic Crisis
A second wave of
economic crisis as
companies go broke.

Will we sink into
economic depression?
The signs are not good.

Yet Harvey Norman Booms
Gerry Harvey has
never sold so much stock, boom
time for Gerry's stores.

NZ Tourist Bubble
South Australia and
New South Wales first to prosper
from Kiwi tourists.

US Debate
Pandemonium
and damaging for the soul
of America.

Day 60 – 2 October

7, 2

Chadstone Cluster Warning
*Chadstone cluster shows
risks of lifting restrictions
too soon*, says Andrews.

Border to Open
Queensland to lower
drawbridge to New South Wales from
November 1st.

And Tassie Too
Tassie opens up
their borders to everyone
except exiled Vics.

Happy Hour
Happy hour for those
in Queensland who can now stand
at a bar and drink.

Feast or Famine
Some businesses are
sacking while others are now
hiring—fickle times.

Contrasting NZ—US Debates
Ardern-Collins were
civil women, Trump-Biden
uber ego men.

Future Presidential Debates
Rule change for debates
because of bad behaviour—
mics will be turned off!

4.30 p.m.—OMG!!!!
Melania and
Trump test positive! Virus
finally got them.

What about Biden?
Has Trump infected him too?
I love irony.

Will conspiracists
say Biden gave it to Trump
to win election?

How will it affect
the election? Will Trump go
into iso? Will

he become very
unwell? It's thrown a spanner
into election.

Will Trump finally
heed the virus's impact?
Such interesting times!

Is it karma or
is there a God? I can't help
my schadenfreude.

It's the Best News
The best corona
news for seven months—and yes,
our thoughts and prayers are ...

Bizarre
Just when the world could
not get more bizarre, it did—
USA psycho.

Interlude—Lifeboat
Trump, Putin, Boris,
Bolsonaro, Duterte,
who to throw out first?

Day 61 – 3 October

8, 3

Under Siege
Dan looks like a man
under siege, drawn, tired eyes,
pale and greying hair.

Warning
Don't risk everything,
warns Prof. Sutton to maskless
Melbourne revellers.

Garden Variety
Theatre to return
to Melbourne's Bot. Gardens with
performances of

music, comedy,
Shakespeare, while indoor venues
might still remain closed.

Trump in Hospital
Another bizarre
day—Trump in hospital for
treatment for virus.

'Unpresidented'
Trump's doctors have now
given him a cocktail of
antibody drugs.

US Train-Wreck
It's the train-wreck you
can't look away from, as it
careers towards doom.

India
100,000
deaths, and virus has exposed
major gaps in care.

Disinformation
Pandemic is ripe
for disinformation spread,
status quo upset.

Day 62 – 4 October

12, 1

Closure of Beaches
Beachside councils in
Melbourne threaten closure if
people overcrowd.

All Eyes
All eyes are on Trump,
we watch on with a morbid,
strange fascination.

Plague-house
White House infected,
key personnel go under,
who will be the next?

It Gets Better—Republican Cluster
The virus is now
going through Republicans
like poop through a goose.

How Unwell?
How unwell is Trump?
Confusion about his health,
fuels speculation.

White Coats Speak
*The president is
doing very well*, say Trump's
men, all in white coats

Trump's Hollow Words
*I have to be back
to make America great
again*, sounds glib now.

Vigils
Trump's supporters are
holding vigils outside the
hospital he's in.

Interlude—Amazon Fires
Lungs of the Earth burn,
the Amazon is on fire.
Deforestation

by ranchers, farmers,
miners with free rein to clear
using fire, the cause.

Day 63 – 5 October

9, 0

Lineball
Prof. Sutton says it
is *lineball* if we move to
step 3 of roadmap

by October 9.
Rolling average of below
five cases per day

will be a very
close call if restrictions are
to be eased further.

Hard to Watch
It's a bit hard to
watch journos grill Andrews—he
looks and sounds tired,

endless questions from
Peta Credlin seeking to
trip Dan up, bugs me.

Dan's Jacket
We haven't seen the
North Face jacket for a while.
So, does it feel snubbed?

Oct 12 Return of Vic. Schools
VCAL, VCE,
year 7 students, special
schools, set to return.

The Trump Show
Shock, irony, then
scepticism, then fury
some sympathy but

now uncertainty.
Is it fake news and is he
really sick? Or is

it a ploy to draw
sympathy, or perhaps he
bides his time before

rebounding, strutting
strength/invincibility
before the nation?

As wild and whacky
as this seems, anything goes
with Trump and his ilk.

Trump Leaves Hospital to Pay
a little surprise
visit to his patriot
supporters. It's all

theatre for effect,
stage-managing his image,
political games.

The drive-by stunt may
have infected people in
his car who will now

have to go into
14-day quarantine. Trump,
the uber hero.

Who Was it Really?
So could it have been
Alec Baldwin posing as
Trump in SUV?

Day 64 – 6 October

15, 1

Stubborn Digits
Bugger, cases count
remains stubborn, and recent
outbreaks need squashing.

Chadstone Cluster
Gargantuan task,
Vic. health worried about the
spike— how to trace them?

Can You Believe It!
Trump leaves hospital
while more staff come down with the
virus, says: *he feels*

*better than he did
20 years ago*—and the
campaign trail beckons.

*Don't be afraid of
COVID*, says Trump. *Don't let it
dominate your life.*

So, tell that to the
millions world-wide who have died,
and tell their loved ones.

Trump's 'Genius'
Fake news and *fake polls*,
discrediting the news—Trump's
stroke of genius

Fourth Estate has been
rendered a paper tiger
after Trump's attacks.

Day 65 – 7 October

6, 2

Ho-hum
Coronacoaster
continues as cases plunge
to single figures.

Corona Budget
Trickle-down budget
aimed to stimulate business
forgets too many.

No social housing,
and a slash to homelessness
funding a big blow.

Treasurer's faith is
in business to actually
create secure jobs.

Budget does not glow
for casuals, unemployed or
the poor who struggle.

Older Job Seekers
Men and women who
are over 35 miss
out in the budget.

Budget Deficit
Nation's gross debt will
be one trillion dollars in
four years—tough times loom.

Tax Cuts
Tax cuts will be brought
forward to put cash in the
pockets of the rich.

Thinking Ahead?
Is the budget a
long term plan or is it just
election tactics?

Kilmore Café
Hundreds of people
are in quarantine after
a café outbreak.

Population
COVID has put the
brakes on population growth
in Victoria.

Railroading
There are fears that Trump
will railroad Big Pharma to
produce quick vaccine.

Trump Tweets
COVID-19 is
far less lethal than the flu,
says super spreader.

Trump's Ego
Egomaniac,
ego as big as the Ritz,
hubris on steroids.

Day 66 – 8 October

11, 0

Pledge
Dan pledges that some
COVID rules will be eased on
October 19th

but as to the scale
of them depends on the case
numbers. We're anxious.

Budget Fears for Women
Women left behind
in budget plan for nation's
restoration with

Labor calling it
a *pink recession and a*
blue recovery.

JobMaker
Government pinning
hopes on JobMaker to get
young folk into jobs.

It Can Happen Anywhere
The Gold Standard State
is having some issues with
growing case numbers.

Gladys frustrated
with businesses not sticking
to the COVID rules.

Screening
Cancer screening rates
have plummeted during the
pandemic crisis.

White House Cluster
Virus continues
to spread through White House, yet Trump
is still cavalier.

Fumigation
White House is empty
while it is fumigated—
who's running the show?

Narcissistic Narrative
Trump hasn't mentioned
Melania or the folks
he has infected.

How are they faring?
It's all about him and his
puffed up, vile, ego.

Day 67 – 9 October

11, 0

Frustration
Numbers plateauing,
frustration for us all—we
want to see movement.

Uphill Battle
It is an uphill
battle to stamp out this pest
of a tricky germ.

Outbreak
Box Hill Hospital
cluster a concern, contact
tracing now in place.

NSW Public Transport
Public transport woes
amid virus spread, with stern
health warnings issued.

Tawdry
Trump soap opera is
tawdrier than *Days of Our
Lives* by a long shot.

Tweet Storm
Unhinged Trump tweets up
late-night storm—what the bloody
hell is going on?

Trivialising
Trump makes light of his
COVID diagnosis, says:
I'm not contagious

and COVID is a
blessing from God. Is there no
end to his hubris?

Reckless
Trump's recklessness is
mind-boggling, he's controlled by
his massive ego.

Is his erratic
conduct the result of the
drug cocktail he's on?

Day 68 – 10 October

14, 0

100 Days of Dan
For 100 days
Dan has stood before us and
delivered bad news.

No Deaths
While cases remain
steady, no deaths have occurred
for three straight days, Yay.

Achilles Heels
Chadstone, Kilmore, Box
Hill—growing outbreaks stand in
way of rules easing.

Lowering Expectation
Dan is preparing
us for more pain by lowering
our expectations.

Disobedience Risk
If Dan doesn't ease
restrictions there's a risk of
disobedience.

Hypocrisy
ScoMo continues
to attack Queensland's border
closure, not Tassie's.

It's politics, as
the Queensland election looms.
Libs are underdogs.

Footy Circus
The footy circus
is drawing to a close—it
has served its purpose.

Still Testing Positive?
Trump returns to the
campaign trail but won't confirm
if he's positive.

Debate Abandoned
Second debate has
been abandoned after Trump
refused the format.

Questions
Questions over Trump's
fitness to hold office are
being asked by some.

Day 69 – 11 October

12, 1

State of Disaster/Emergency
has been extended
to November 8th as a
precaution by Dan.

CHO Prof. Sutton Warning
We may have *to live
with 10 to 15 cases,
zero will be hard.*

More Bizarre
It gets more and more
bizarre in America,
Trump's soap opera rules.

Another QAnon Conspiracy
Trump is pretending
to be sick as part of his
plan to, yes, arrest

Hillary Clinton
over her part in a ring
of paedophiles who

worship Satan. And
Republicans running for
office believe this!

First Rally Since
Trump tells invited
supporters *the virus is
disappearing.* While

no one in the crowd
was wearing a mask nor was
Trump—stupid or what?

350,766 Deaths
across the world in
one death-filled day, which is a
new tragic record.

Day 70 – 12 October

15, 0

Pressure from ScoMo and Josh
Pressure to open
up Vic.—we're Danned if we do
and Danned if we don't.

Is It reasonable?
Is pressure on Dan
reasonable? He wants to
avoid a third wave.

Mounting Business Disquiet
A challenge to Dan's
lockdown validity is
mounted in High Court.

Hotel Inquiry
It's looking messy
for Dan, as pressure builds. Do
all roads lead to him?

No Good News
Retail unlikely
to hear any good news on
Sunday from Andrews.

Take Heed
Australia could do
well to take heed of Europe's
second wave outbreak.

Lost Their Surplus Edge
Libs have lost their edge,
with the surplus gone, and now
Albo's got some bite.

London
Restrictions will be
ramped up—cases surge, travel
to be limited.

Superman
Self-styled Superman,
Trump claims he is *immune*. Bring
on the Kryptonite!

Spin Doctor Declares
Trump declares: *I can't
get it. I can't give it.* The
spin doctor preaches.

Gladys' Trouble
Gladys' boyfriend
caught doing dodgy deals—how
will this now play out?

Their relationship
revealed, her integrity
and judgement questioned.

Day 71 – 13 October

12, 1

10.30 a.m. — No Confidence Vote
Michael O'Brien
to move no confidence vote
in parliament. Stunt?

Slightly Up
Rolling day average
slightly up— what will this mean
for our hard lockdown?

Vic. Mysteries
Mystery infections,
a key to further steps, were
also up again.

Longest and Hardest
Melbourne's endured the
longest and hardest lockdown
of any locale.

Redrawing Vic. Roadmap
Roadmap is to be
redrawn because of the harm
caused by restrictions.

How?
How on earth is Dan
still standing after months of
such intensity?

Eccles Gone
Top public servant
has resigned—a casualty
of quarantine probe.

COVID Fines Not Paid
A fraction of the
COVID fines issued by the
police have been paid.

Maybe Dan needs to
assess who has been fined—the
disadvantaged/poor?

No Resignation
Gladys refuses
to resign over puzzling
tryst with shamed MP.

She may have had poor
judgement with him but is she
then a bad leader?

Tally Topping
New South Wales tops Vic.
again in daily cases,
some cluster worries.

Trump Negative
White House physician
says Trump's tested negative,
he's not infectious.

Humble Trump?
*I'm so energised
by your prayers and humbled by
your support.* At a

massive rally, with
YMCA blaring. Trump
says he would like to

plunge into the crowd
and give voters *a big fat
kiss*. Trump merch was for

sale, while face masks were
absent. Trump was shouting: *I
feel so powerful!*

Day 72 – 14 October

7, 5

Breaking News!
83 per cent
of people just want COVID
to go away, now.

East Coast Scandals
Three leaders face a
day of reckoning: Gladys,
Dan and Frecklington.

The Knives are Out
Dan had better watch
his back—media, colleagues,
opponents, have knives.

House of Cards Falling?
Is Dan's house of cards
about to fall under the
weight of a failure?

Contact Tracing Lessons
Has Victoria
learned its lesson with contact
tracing, is it fixed?

My Diary's Mental Health
My diary is sick,
it is depressed and has now
withdrawn from the world.

Each page for each day
is blank—forlorn days ahead.
My diary's queasy,

it's not well, and it
all stems from deep internal
trauma from neglect.

It needs therapy
from someone who understands
diary essentials.

Perhaps Deep Dialogue
or meditation can help
it to find meaning.

Medication won't
work and I wouldn't dare give
it ECT, but

some good CBT
may do the trick and restore
its self-esteem. And

who knows, the days may
suddenly fill up with lots
of appointments. Yes

full recovery
is possible with the right
treatment and support.

A Piece of the MCG for GF
Hallowed turf has been
dug up from the G's goal square,
sent to the Gabba.

Symbolic
Our mandatory masks
are a sign of our bondage
to this damn virus.

COVID Sanity
These haikus are my
COVID sanity, a way
to process the crap

and ironically
the madder the world becomes
the saner I am!

In fact, this crazy
world makes my madness look like
the tamest creature.

Message to Trump
You cannot build a
country on narcissism
and rage. Take heed mate.

Day 73 – 15 October

6, 0

Please be Honest
Authorities plead
with people to be honest
with contact tracers.

From One Person
400 people
now in isolation through
one person's actions.

It's Tough in Melbourne
We're doing it tough
here and our humour seems to
be ebbing away.

Doubts
Doubts are creeping in—
are we on the right path in
managing this thing?

The Magic Number
We may not reach the
magic number of five—might
need to reassess.

Dan: We're Closer
Dan promises: *we're
closer to COVID normal*
as case numbers dip.

Shepparton
Testing places in
Shepparton overwhelmed as
virus worry spreads.

Gladys' Ex
Gladys' ex is
accused of being corrupt
as all hell. Bad choice?

Day 74 – 16 October

2, 0

Something Promising
Praise be the Lord! The
numbers are finally in
our favour at last.

Unpick a Stitch
How are Dan and Prof.
Sutton getting on? A slight
bit of tension there?

The garment starts to
fray at the edges before
it unravels. Is

Dan now a villain
after being a hero?
Unpick a stitch and …

100 Days
since Dan called the *State
of Disaster*. It's been a
hard time for Melbourne.

Gangbusters
Virus is going
gangbusters in Europe and
UK—cases soar

WHO says: *evolving
epidemic in Europe
raises great concern.*

Media Frenzy
Is the media
frenzy around Gladys fair?
Are they hounding her?

US Election TV Appearances
Trump belligerent,
Biden doddery and lame,
both uninspiring.

Trump peddles 'greatness'
and nothing else. Biden tries
to show steadfastness.

Out of the millions
of people in the US,
Trump and Biden are

White House candidates.
Surely, they can do better
than these dismal men?

Day 75 – 17 October

1, 0

Tomorrow's News
Dan says there will be
some easing of restrictions
tomorrow—we wait.

Interstate Travel
Regional Vics are
close to being able to
travel interstate.

Amazing Time
It's an amazing
time, watching how world leaders
manage the virus.

Addictive Theatre
Dan's daily updates
are addictive viewing, like
all good theatre is

they have become the
most watched television show—
Dan the mega star!

NZ Travellers Bubble Burst
Trans-Tasman travel
bubble has been breached on its
first day by travellers

who have flown into
Melbourne. Where the hell are they?
Who has bungled this?

Trump is Moving
*heaven and earth to
protect all seniors from the
'China' virus.* Sure.

Boris' NDE
Boris kept shaking
hands, downplaying the risks of
the virus, until

he was infected,
landing in ICU on
a ventilator.

Johnson's NDE
rejigged his take on virus.
Trump could learn from him.

Alcohol Consumption
Effects of COVID
has seen increase in women
drinking alcohol.

After Being In
lockdown for seven
months, we may have forgotten
how to socialise.

Was It a Scam?
No one's recovered
so quickly from the virus
as Trump did. So, did

he really have it?
Or was it a scam to fool
some of the people?

Day 76 – 18 October

2, 0

9.45 a.m. – D-Day
Well, it's D-Day for
Melburnians, as we wait
for Andrews to speak.

11.30 a.m. – Dan Speaks
Travel radius—
25 kilometres,
tennis courts, skate parks

golf courses are to
open as can hairdressers.
Two-hour limit for

outdoor exercise
and socialising will be
scrapped, and two households

can meet outside in
groups of ten. Home maintenance
can resume, as can

pet grooming, outdoor
photography. There is more
freedom for regions.

Another slate of
welcome changes will come on
November 1st.

Blow
Disappointed. Was
wanting more freedom, but hey,
look at overseas.

Job Seekers
Those on JobSeeker
applying for a job, are
up against hundreds.

Footy Circus Grand Final
Cats and Tigers are
set to play off in GF.
Miracle season?

Brownlow Medal Tonight
A virtual Brownlow
Medal count—new format for
this pandemic world.

POTUS and FLOTUS
POTUS runs amok
across America, but
where is dear FLOTUS?

Defying Experts
Trump plans to hold a
mass rally in Wisconsin
against all advice.

Day 77 – 19 October

4, 1

Count Down
Counting down the days,
patiently waiting for Dan's
next proclamation.

Weary
I am weary of
my isolation, my mind
wanders to beyond.

Brownlow Winner
Lion King Neale takes
home Charlie, after leaving
the field in his wake.

Furious Josh
Josh launches broadside
at *bloody-minded* Dan and
his cautious easing.

COVID Hub
We're living in our
Reeves Road COVID Hub where I
feel safe and peaceful.

Trans-Tasman Bubble Anger
Anger from Dan at
NZ travellers entering
Vic. against wishes.

Getting Nasty
Shift in tone from the
pollies—nasty name-calling
and allegations.

Why do they have to
divide and conquer? Where's the
cooperation?

Day 78 – 20 October

1, 0

Raising Expectations
Dan is now raising
our expectations—pledging
significant steps

as case numbers fall.
For lockdown-weary Vics, it's
the best news in months.

Hotel Quarantine Inquiry
Prof. Sutton asked to
provide affidavit, is
he the next to go?

Watching the Footy GF
Sadly, people won't
be able to gather in
groups to watch the game.

'Shear' Joy
The clack of scissors
once again fills the rooms of
barbers and salons.

Frydenberg Again
accuses Andrews
of a *callous indifference*
to small businesses

and Dan responds: *He's
not a leader, he's just a
Liberal.* So there, Josh.

Shadow Pandemic
Record number of
victims of family violence
seeking help, has put

pressure on those who
work in the sector, causing
case-worker burnout.

Interstate Rivalry
It's a tale of two
cities—Melbourne and Sydney
and the pandemic.

215,000 Dead
and Trump says people
are now *tired of hearing
Fauci and all these*

idiots who are
warning of the dangers of
COVID-19, and

of a time that is
now *disturbingly anti-
science* in essence.

Europe—150,000 New Daily Cases
Record spike in the
number of cases across
Continent concerns.

Remdesivir
Jury still out on
the drug Trump claims cured him.
Trials are ongoing.

Racking up the Numbers
40 million world-
wide cases, one million dead,
the numbers don't lie.

Day 79 – 21 October

3, 0

Crisis Looms
Homelessness crisis
looms as crucial supports from
government drop off.

99 Per Cent of Victoria's
second wave can be
traced back to two hotels set
up for quarantine.

Missing Vibe
This strange feeling of
Melbourne missing the vibe of
our Grand Final Week.

Abandoning Public Transport
Infection fears could
result in more cars flooding
roads, causing gridlock.

Northcote Golf Course Spat
Locals used course for
recreation while it was
closed to golfers, now

golfers want it back,
while the public want to keep
the land as a park.

Day of Our Little COVID Lives
Our lives shrink even
smaller, where the rustle of
leaves is a big thing.

Were our *big* lives a
delusion before we were
grounded by COVID?

Church Pressure
New South Wales buckles
on virus rules after some
pressure from churches.

Obscene Election Money
The obscene amount
of money Biden and Trump
are spending, appals.

Trump's Lie
America is
crushing coronavirus.
Lies, lies and more lies.

Trump's Feud
Trump's feud with Fauci
not a good look with voters
before election.

How is FLOTUS?
Trump is crisscrossing
America, desperate to
win votes, but meanwhile

Melania is
at home and still suffering from
her bout of COVID.

Day 80 – 22 October

5, 0

New Cluster Fears
Thousands targeted
in testing blitz after a
school's positive case

fuelling fears of a
a new outbreak in northern
suburbs of Melbourne.

Weekend Drones
Vic. police will use
drones to survey footy crowds,
big brother's watching?

Trolling Magda
Magda targeted
by extremists after her
COVID ad for Dan.

ACT
ACT records
its first COVID case in more
than 100 days.

What Else?
Drought, bushfires, global
pandemic and recession,
what else can happen?

Not Cashed Up
Donald Trump struggling
for cash, as campaign reaches
the final stretch. Yay.

Post-Modern President
Were we groomed for an
alternative facts, fake news
president by post-

modernism and
its snub of the idea of
an ultimate truth?

Obama Denounces Trump
Trump hasn't shown that
he has any interest in
doing the work or

helping anyone.
It's not a reality
show. Self-obsessed Trump

isn't going to
protect all of us, he can't
protect himself. So

the Trump horror show
rolls on, with him tweeting at
the television

making up stuff to
fool people into thinking
he's governing them.

Greatest Democracy?
When people are not
able to register to
vote and money rules,

and voting is on
a working day and queues are
long—democracy?

Meanwhile, Trump prepares
the electorate for what he
says is going to

be a fraudulent
election if he loses.
He is sowing the

seeds of dissent and
anti-democratic rule—
his militia waits.

Day 81 – 23 October

1, 0

Optimism
Optimism is
growing that restrictions will
be eased on Sunday.

Melbourne's Northern Outbreak
500 people
have been told to isolate
after fresh outbreak.

Christmas Opening of Border
Christmas timeline as
National Cabinet agrees
on a plan with all

the states bar Western
Australia who will keep their
border closed. While the

premiers will make their
own decisions and wear the
costs of their actions.

Protests Again
300 maskless
people gather at the Shrine
to protest lockdown.

Europe's Second Wave
Hospital systems
are at risk of buckling as
continent is hit.

A widespread virus-
fatigue, and economic
impact, have worn down

public support for
lockdowns, so governments are
trying to balance

the need to keep the
economy turning while
halting the virus.

No Dog
Trump is the only
president ever not to
have a White House dog.

Day 82 – 24 October

7, 0

Restless Night
After a restless
night, what grim news will I wake
to in the morning?

9.30 a.m. – Footy Grand Final Day
Well, we got there, the
Grand Final is tonight, yes,
miracles happen.

The Gabba hosts the
first final under lights as
Tigers and Cats clash.

So, I'll settle in
with chocolate and a Diet
Coke and watch the game.

For the First Time There
will be a bigger
crowd at NRL final
than the AFL.

Pending Results
Pending test results
will shape much of tomorrow's
statement on guidelines.

The Arts
So how will the arts
emerge from the pandemic?
Stronger or weaker?

If a poet put
on a high-vis vest, hard hat,
maybe they'd be seen.

Will the arts ever
return in all its glory?
We sooo need artists.

WHO Warns
the world is at a
critical juncture, as the
virus is spreading

faster than the first
wave, and Britain and Europe
are in deep trouble.

Russian Interference
Interference by
Russia in America's
election is an

attempt to destroy
our faith in democracy
and all it stands for.

Day 83 – 25 October

7, 0

The Circus Is Over
The circus ended
last night, the Tigers reigning
supreme over Cats.

What will we do now
without the distraction of
AFL footy?

11 a.m. – Waiting for Test Results
Dan's waiting for test
results from Northern Melbourne
before more easing.

Disappointed Dan
says we need to get on top
of cluster in north.

We need a *cautious
pause* while we are waiting for
the information.

Patience Wearing Thin
People's patience is
wearing thin, we are desperate
for our liberty.

Blow to Business
The *cautious pause* is
a blow to business who are
keen to open up.

Slowly Springing Back to Life
Melbourne is slowly
springing back to life— barbers,
skateboarders are back.

Victorians Are Divided
on support for State
easing restrictions, though most
support *ring of steel*.

Mikakos Weighs in
accusing Dan of
having *paralysis in
decision-making*.

6.30 p.m. — Results Are In
1,000 tests have
come back negative so far,
good news for cluster.

Are We Ready for Third Wave?
Would Australia be
ready for a third wave if
or when it happened?

Final Stretch
The final stretch of
the USA election
is colliding with

a surge in virus
cases and mass admissions
to the hospitals.

Trump insists they are
rounding the corner on the
virus. *When we win*

you won't hear about
COVID anymore. It is
going away. The

sheer madness of his
head-in-the-sand blows my mind,
it's astonishing!

Day 84 – 26 October

0, 0

Zero, Zero
Beautiful numbers,
zero cases, zero deaths,
can I hold some hope?

It's been a long time,
139
days since no cases.

3.30 p.m.—Announcement
IT'S TIME!
Emotional Dan
brings Vic's marathon shutdown
to an end with the

city to open
up again—restaurants, cafés,
hotels, bars, all with

limits on numbers
inside and outside. Tuesday
is Opening Day.

After 15 weeks
of a hard lockdown the news
was very welcome

but with our freedom
comes responsibility
to do the right thing.

Checkpoint Charlie
Challenging going
through the checkpoint at Coldstream,
something from Cold War.

The Other Final
Melbourne Storm hold off
Penrith Panthers to win the
NRL final.

#FakeMelania
Social media
rife with speculation of
a FLOTUS double.

US—83,000 Infections
in a single day.
Trump doesn't want to mention
the surge in COVID.

Pence's Staff
Mike Pence's staff test
positive—White House cluster
shows stupidity.

Day 85 – 27 October

0, 0

Thank You
Plaudits flood in from
the nation—Victorians
get big pat on back

for toughing out the
hardest of lockdowns, the most
trying of times, but

no one is thanking
Dan for resisting ScoMo
and Josh's carping,

calling on him to
open up sooner, they put
enormous pressure

on Dan, as did the
business folks, but he hung in,
and was led by the

data, health advice.
So, I thank Dan for staying
the course, holding hope.

Support for Dan
In spite of all that
has happened, support is still
strong for Dan, whereas

for the *assistant
librarian* O'Brien,
support is lacking.

Harping and carping
hasn't cut the mustard with
we Victorians.

From Dan
To Melburnians—
a tribute *to* your *courage,
kindness, commitment.*

Supermarket Cheering
Yesterday at a
supermarket, it was put
over the PA

by the manager,
that there were zero cases,
shoppers cheered loudly.

Victoria-Baiting
It has become a
thing—Victoria-baiting—
among Fed. pollies

who once said: *we are
in this together,* yet they
twisted the dagger

when Victoria
was on its knees, nit-picked Dan,
made us feel alone.

Frydenberg Unloads Again
Josh unloads on Dan
yet again in parliament—
politics shits me.

Comparison
Victoria and
Britain in similar place
12 weeks ago, now

Vic. has zero new
cases while Britain today
has 20,000.

Day 86 – 28 October

2, 2

11.59 p.m. Last Night
Vics queuing up at
midnight at cafés for their
first taste of freedom,

the atmosphere was
electric—people dying
to have a few beers.

Some Rules
Home restrictions are
still in place to stop family
virus transmission.

Ring of Steel
Ring of steel between
Melbourne and regions will be
lifted very soon.

Don't Blow It
Now that restrictions
have eased, we must abide by
COVID safety rules.

Dan Pleads
*Please, please, do not go
crazy,* as sudden freedom
turns people loco.

Out of Stage 4
Roadmap out of Stage
4 begins with sizable
easing of the rules.

Essential Reasons Removed
The four essential
reasons to leave home have been
scrapped—freedom at last!

**Interlude—4.30 p.m.
Announcement of 2020 Victorian
Community History Awards**
What a crazy year,
in amongst the dross our book
wins history award!

Day 87 – 29 October

2, 0

Curve Flattened
Regional Vic. has
zero active cases—so
the curve has flattened.

Corruption at V/Line
uncovered with a
contractor pocketing dosh.
Corruption in spades

such as deep cleaning
on metro trains not being
done then covered up.

US Election
Misinformation
spreading like wildfire across
the United States

such as Trump *ended
the COVID pandemic*, claim
made by Ivanka.

Under Attack
Trump under attack
from all sides—he incites a
politics of hate.

Second Wave Trouble for Europe
Germany and France
bring in curfews and lockdowns
as virus invades.

While Germany was
victorious in round one
now round two begins.

Much vaunted test and
trace system overwhelmed by
rampant pandemic.

Is Boris watching
over the channel to see
what is happening?

Europe may have a
COVID festive season like
no other, poor things.

Day 88 – 30 October

4, 0

No Dan
Dan ends marathon,
121
days of his briefings.

Dan will not attend
tomorrow's COVID-19
daily press conference.

Palaszczuk's Border Call
Queensland remains off
limits to Sydneysiders
and Victorians.

Gladys says Queensland's
border standards are too high,
not driven by health

advice, rather the
upcoming election which
Labor hopes to win.

Border Surprise
Western Australia
names date to take down its much
vaunted hard border.

Triaged
Dangerous times when
hospitals are overrun,
patients start to be

triaged, selected
to live or die, ethical
choices for doctors

who hold life and death,
in their hands. A cruel virus
that sees elderly

and the disabled
first to be cut loose—Europe
returns to this place.

Frantic Last Dash
The frantic last dash
for the White House is in full
swing as Trump barnstorms.

Day 89 – 31 October

0, 0

Grieving
Melbourne opens up,
but there are COVID scars and
grief is everywhere.

Lethal Virus
COVID-19 is
so lethal that even the
Reaper wears a mask.

The Prof. Says
we have earned the right
to *enjoy ourselves now*—it's
been such a long haul.

Looking Back
How will we look back
on this time when everything
changed and time stood still?

Trump Accuses Doctors
Trump claims: *our doctors
get more money if someone
dies from COVID*. Sure.

91,248 New Cases
US astounds with
soaring cases. Trump doesn't
want to mention it.

Differences
Biden warns of tough
days ahead, Trump lives in his
denial bubble.

UK Deaths
UK in trouble,
200 deaths reported
every day this week

and 10,000 in
hospital, the NHS
buckles under stress.

Day 90 – 1 November

0, 0

Australia Wide
Yay, for the first time in five months, there were no new cases reported.

Palaszczuk Victory
Palaszczuk sweeps back into power in Queensland on back of COVID.

PR
A desperate PR campaign by Trump to find some celebrities to

help his election, has failed miserably at taxpayers' expense.

Barricades and Boards
Businesses in New York board-up windows and the police put up steel barricades, just in case there is election-day turmoil from vote count.

Lesson Learned?
Boris: *we need to be humble in the face of nature,* hard lesson.

580,000 People
are contracting the
virus in a week across
large parts of England.

*Unless we act, we
could see deaths in this country
running at several*

thousand a day, says
panicked Boris who's about
to lockdown England.

The Prince of Shambles
is charged with making the same
mistake twice, of not

closing England down
quick enough to save lives, as
health and money clash.

He must navigate
the tightrope leaders are faced
with, in this time of

global pandemic,
and the widespread misery
it has brought, meanwhile

suicide, mental
illness, poverty, despair,
grip Merry England.

Less Paper Used
Working from home sees
a sharp decline in paper
used in offices.

Day 91 – 2 November

0, 0

The Silent Cup
Melbourne Cup with no
crowd may benefit horses
who are spooked by crowds,

we'll hear the horses
hooves, jockeys yelling, urging
their horses to win.

Queensland Voted
Has Pauline Hanson's
populism run out of
puff as the voting

for One Nation in
Queensland has collapsed like a
house of shoddy cards?

Incumbents have an
advantage, oppositions
struggle not to sound

negative for which
they are punished. How can they
remain relevant?

As major parties
struggle to get traction, fringe
parties fade away.

2020 is
not a normal year, things are
in a state of flux.

Prince William Infected
Wills was infected
with virus in April but
kept it a secret,

he had a severe
case, struggled to breathe. Even
a prince can succumb.

Climate Change
Unchecked climate change
tipped to dwarf the impact of
COVID recession.

Fear of Going Out
Our COVID bubble
is familiar, while we are
emotionally

exhausted after
lockdown, will leaving it cause
some of us to have

anxiety and
a bad case of FOGO where
we are more cautious.

Joy of Going Out
So, can we all re-
discover JOGO after
our prolonged lockdown?

Fear of Missing Out
And will FOMO come
back to us as we start to
be more sociable?

So
will FOGO put paid
to FOMO or will JOGO
re-enter our lives?

No Panacea
The election of
Biden crucial, hygienic,
but hardly hopeful

because it may not
remedy America's
deeply ingrained plight.

Election Shenanigans
Will Trump claim early
victory and challenge postal
votes in Supreme Court?

Planning for Bedlam
The existential
crisis of America
will come to a head

on election day.
Trump's militia wait in the
wings to unleash their

fury if Trump does
lose. Bedlam beckons, as the
country tears itself

apart, while many
regret voting for Trump last
time only to see

his narcissism
hold the whole country hostage.
We didn't plan on

a psychopath in
the White House, laments someone
who voted for Trump

and will now vote for
Biden and risk dividing
her family, like so

much of the country,
where social madness takes hold
and the nightmare fumes.

Trump Rallies Collateral
30,000 were
infected, 700
estimated dead.

On Second Thoughts
America makes
Bedlam look like the sanest
place on this planet!

Day 92 – 3 November

0, 0

Prof. Sutton—The Quaddie
This is the quaddie
we wanted. 0,0,0,0
four days of zero.

Exodus
Melburnians leave
city in record numbers
in the June quarter.

Protective Femininity
Female leaders put
people's health first: Palaszczuk,
Ardern, Merkel and

Solberg, who have all
been compassionate and, yes,
authoritative.

Trump's Bible
Trump swore allegiance
to US on his bible—
The Art of the Deal.

Guns
Americans have
bought 17 million guns
in the past few weeks!

'Fire Fauci'
Trump hints he will fire
Fauci post-election if
he wins—a bad move?

Biden's Barb
*First step to beating
the virus is beating Trump.*
Joe supports Fauci.

Trump Complains
*I've been under siege
illegally for three-and-
a-half-years.* says Trump.

The Polls
Biden leads polls but
I don't trust Americans
who are spooked by Trump.

Election Whistle-Stop
It's the magical
egotistical tour of
one Donald J. Trump.

White House Ring of Steel
White House protected
by a ring of steel in case
of voting chaos.

UN Observers
If the US was
a developing country,
its election would

be monitored by
UN observers, to make
sure it's above board.

Day 93 – 4 November

0, 0

9.45 a.m.—We Wait
We wait for the count
of votes in America
while fearing the worst.

Count Our Blessings
As the world falls to
the virus again, we count
our blessing and thank

our leaders for their
vigilance in keeping us
safe against the odds

yes, Dan, Gladys and
the rest, have taken some tough
decisions in the

face of stern dissent.
We could be France, the UK,
America, Spain.

Our zero figures
are hard won so we must not
court complacency.

Cup Day Revellers
Crowded beaches and
people flouting COVID rules
frustrates premier who

urges us to keep
following the set guidelines.
What we have achieved

is fragile and it's
precious and if we don't play
our part, it won't last.

23 November Border to Open
Vics will be welcomed
again in New South Wales as
Gladys lets us in.

Paris Infection Horror
One Parisian
infected every twenty
seconds by virus.

4.30 p.m.
Election is tight
on a knife's edge—so will Trump
win a nail-bitter?

White House Madhouse
Will Americans
vote to keep insanity
in White House madhouse?

Without Incidents
Election day went
largely without incident
amidst unrest fears.

Trump Tweet
Concerns are for *due
process* after Trump tweet calls
to *stop counting votes*.

Trump in Contention?
Unfolding mess in
US as Trump vote surge puts
him in contention.

6.30 p.m.
Trump stands in front of
a forest of flags and says,
we're gonna win big.

Enraged, he calls the
election *a fraud* and *an
embarrassment* and

declares Democrats
are *stealing* the election,
votes disappearing,

claims skulduggery.
So, Trump's off to the Supreme
Court to lodge appeals.

Here's the Rub
Trump encouraged his
supporters to go and vote
in person, while the

Democrats, with the
virus in mind, said do a
a postal vote as

it will be safer.
Trump says these votes shouldn't be
counted, aren't legal.

Tell that to all the
folks who postal voted in
good faith, legally.

Biden Cautious
Biden cautiously
says he is on track to claim
victory and asks

everyone to be
*patient and let the votes be
counted* as they should.

9.00 p.m.
I go to bed dark
and solemn, not knowing what
I will wake to in

the morning, or how
geo-politics across
the world will play out.

Putin and Jinping
will love watching the US
fold into itself

and to witness how
fragile democracy is
under Trump's strange reign.

Trump or Biden? The
tribe is divided, but Trump
is bullish, claims win.

We may have a long
wait before there's a result—
American pain.

QAnon in House
Marjorie Greene, a
QAnon supporter, wins
a seat in Congress!

Day 94 – 5 November

0, 0

Cheering
Victorians are
cheering the continuing
double doughnut days.

Vaccines Agreement
AstraZeneca
vaccine to be rolled out in
first quarter next year.

Free Again
Victorians could
be free to travel any
where in Australia

by December, as
low numbers pave the way for
a tourism boom.

7.30 a.m.
Meanwhile Back in the USA
False Claim
Trump's false claim of a
victory may have come too
soon, Joe Biden looms.

Wrong Again
Polls got it wrong. No
Biden landslide, pundits with
egg on their faces.

Unbelievable
For all of Trump's bad
handling of the virus, they
still voted for him.

Staggering 108,000
new cases in the
US yesterday. Not once
did Trump, during the

campaign, express his
thoughts and prayers for those who have
died from the virus.

Fears
Many fear for the
democratic process in
the United States.

Some call Trump's actions
reckless and dangerous and
irresponsible.

8.40 a.m.
Biden may pull it
off, as a few swing states start
now to fall this way.

Trump Cult
Republicans have
been turned into a cult, ruled
by the Trump family.

Can't Abiden
Trump can't abiden
that he might lose control of
the presidency.

12.20 p.m.
Joe Biden edges
closer—one state away from
magical number.

5 p.m.—Unrest
Anxiety and
suspicion linger in post-
election US.

Unrest on streets builds,
those for *count every vote*, and
those for *stop counting*.

Trump's assertion of
irregularities in
the vote seems to lack

merit, as he goes
on twitter to whip up his
aggrieved followers.

His cynical and
pre-planned strategy, to try
and discredit late

Democrat surge in
the votes, is a dangerous
move to subvert the

democratic will.
When will his party say: *Trump,
enough is enough?*

Tin Helmets
Fetch your tin helmets
as Trump sets in motion some
ill-fated events.

Limbo
Americans are
stuck in a volatile, crass,
limbo, they're angry,

hurting, uncertain
as they watch their country go
to the dogs. So sad.

Biden Wants to Unite USA
Here, the people rule.
We need to unite, to heal,
to come together.

6.30 p.m. – Cynical Power
Trumps wants to halt the
counting of votes in states where
he's losing, but where

he's winning, he wants
counting speeded up. Two-faced,
false and treacherous.

Trump the Spin Doctor
He has managed to
spin the virus in spite of
the massive death-toll.

Pollies around the
world will be watching Trump and
emulating him.

Praise the Gods Australia
Praise the Gods for our
rational voting system—
it makes the US

look like the wild west.
At least we all vote and the
votes are all counted!

Needs Therapy
The American
psyche's sick and needs urgent
psychotherapy.

Day 95 – 6 November

0, 0

Compare the Pair
As America's
cases skyrocket, we have
another doughnut.

Vaccine Manufacture
Australia begins
the manufacture of a
vaccine before it

has been approval by
the TGA—it must go
through the final trials.

Compelling
We've all been transfixed
by the US election,
compelling viewing.

Desperado
Desperate Trump, who will
do anything to win, is
trying to stop count.

Power-hungry, he'd
even trash democracy
to stay in power.

Victim?
Trump plays the victim
when things don't go his way, a
very poor loser?

Stay Patient
Biden still urging
all his supporters *to stay
patient and stay calm.*

Hyperbole
Trump is getting more
desperate, hyperbolic talk,
accusations fly,

he's starting to sound
unhinged, he cannot bear that
he might lose the race.

Pathetic Trump, who's
telling lie after lie, while
watching the lights go

out on his control
as President, clutching at
legal straws. We watch

the soap opera with
our jaws flat on the ground—how
did it come to this?

9.15 p.m. – Georgia
Biden takes the lead
in Georgia which may be the
final blow to Trump.

Day 96 – 7 November

0, 0

Keeps on Coming
The good news for Vics
keeps coming, doughnut again,
good news tomorrow?

Freedom Day?
We are hoping that
Dan rewards our patience and
good will with freedom.

10 am: Biden for President
Joe edges ahead in
in key states and is in line
to win the White House.

Reality Check
Trump's 'Reality
Show' suddenly became real
and Liberty is

standing on her plinth
telling Trump: *you're fired!* And breathes
a sigh of relief.

Embarrassment
Trump's rant from the White
House turned off by news networks
because of untruths

an embarrassment
for the President who has
devalued the brand.

Tainted
Republicans have
to distance themselves from Trump's
Cuckoo's Nest, lest they

be tainted by his
madness, which is destroying
their integrity.

The Trump Lie Detector
Four years, 25
thousand lies, and now in this
election campaign

it's been hard to keep
up with the sheer volume of
Trump's blatant untruths

and he has managed
to normalise lying so
that we expect it.

2.45 p.m.
Biden ahead, he's
tantalisingly close in
four crucial swing states.

121,504 New Cases Yesterday
and still Trump will not
give the virus due respect,
don't mention the war.

God Bless Big America
It is the biggest
democracy and has the
biggest pandemic.

3.45 p.m.
Biden thinks he's won,
but not yet claiming victory—
patience and process.

Delusions of Grandeur
Deluded Trump still
thinks he can win and will take
us to hell to win.

Day 97 — 8 November

0, 0

11 a.m.—Dan Speaks—Approaching COVID Normal
Ring of steel to go
25-kilometre
limit scrapped—*we are*

once again one state.
More people can gather in
restaurants, pubs, cafés

and within families.
Religious ceremony
numbers increased, while

theatres, cinemas,
gyms, indoor sports centres and
libraries open with

limits, but masks and
working from home rules remain
as a precaution.

State of Disaster
to go, *Emergency* to
still remain in place.

New slogan for us,
it is: *stay safe, stay open.*
We have come so far.

Tentative Steps
We'll take tentative
steps back into the world but
with FOGO in mind

fear stalks us as the
virus hasn't suddenly
disappeared—it lurks

For Granted
We had taken so
much for granted—jobs, hugging,
seeing family and

friends, playing music,
sport, going to concerts, shops,
walking in the park

going to playgrounds,
all done once without question,
but to lose all that

was traumatic. I
am now mindful of what can
be taken away

in a heartbeat—life
is tenuous, nothing is
certain anymore.

And Now Back to the USA
4 a.m.
Trump tweets from golf course:
I won this election by
a lot. Wrong, Wrong, Wrong.

5.30 a.m.
Biden elected!
Trump refuses to concede,
hell bent on stalling.

Dancing in the Street
People gathered and
were dancing in the street, high
on hope with Trump gone

but the main mood was
one of relief, after four
years of Trump chaos.

History Made
Kamala Harris,
first black woman to hold the
Vice-Presidency

spoke of listening to
truth and science, blazing the
trail, healing the rifts.

Outpouring
These incredible
scenes would never happen here
with an election

it's as though they are
waking up from a bad dream,
throwing off their chains.

12.30 p.m. – Biden Pledges
to defeat despair,
govern for all, unify,
beat the pandemic.

Meanwhile
Trump beats the war drums,
shows no signs of accepting
the reality.

Hokus Pokus POTUS
Election outcome
Hokus Pokus, says POTUS,
fake votes, fake result.

Cheat
They say never trust
a man who cheats at golf. Guess,
then, who cheats at golf?

No More Twitter Storms
No more 3 a.m.
twitter storms from the leader
who governed by tweet.

Trump's Legacy
What legacy will
Trump leave? This man with a dark
charisma who holds

white, disgruntled men
in the palm of his hands while
promising them the

greatness they crave. This
Faustian character who
sold his soul to the

corporate money kings
while many of his people
live in poverty,

this man, who cannot
accept the people's will and
is undignified

in a defeat he
can't bring himself to admit.
What's left of this man

and his fake orange
face, fake hair, fake politics,
this sad, man of straw

who strutted the stage
like a king, who is Lear
beset by madness,

watching his house of
cards cave in around him? While
we witness his fall

we will wonder what
forces brought him to power,
how he garnered such

popularity,
held America captive
to his hopelessness

and paranoia.
What will history say about
Trump's short, bizarre reign?

Biden's Message
*Make America
respected again* as he
rejects Trumpism.

It's Over
*The long dark night is
over*, now to heal the heart
of a broken land.

Day 98 – 9 November

0, 0

A False Sense of Security
Nine days of zero
not the same as a vaccine.
Don't be lulled into …

First Day
Left home, went shopping
at Officeworks, just like a
regular person

and in my pocket
a new essential item—
have mask will travel.

The God of Destruction
Shiva must go, the
God who kept his people in
apprehension, who

holds us all hostage
to his power hunger. A
brooding Shiva, who

America has
to purge from her soul, must go,
so the wounds can heal.

But what final bit
of destruction will Shiva
wreak on the US?

Will Biden's *better*
angels prevail over a
mad, wrathful Shiva?

Day 99 – 10 November

0, 0

State of Emergency
is extended to
6 December so that
rules can be enforced.

American Psycho
It's getting messy,
Trump Show moves to Cuckoo's Nest
where he hunkers down

like a mad king who
feeds off perverse power. It's
unedifying.

He's firing staff left,
right and centre, triggering
chaos, and now he's

refusing to let
his people speak to Biden's
transition people.

This petulant, lame-
duck will make life difficult
for Americans.

Biden's Battle
Joe Biden's battle
is convincing Trump's voters
that *he* actually

won the election;
that Trump sits on a throne of
lies and he must go.

Liar, Liar
Being branded a
liar for Trump did not bring
stigma, he revelled

in *alternative
facts* and his own *fake news*—the
casualty is truth.

While Rome Burns
And so, Trump plays golf
while America burns—a
reckless lack of care.

Vaccine Stampede
Can a world vaccine-
sharing programme prevent the
marginalised and

the poor from being
trampled by the rich in the
stampede for vaccines?

Day 100 – 11 November and Beyond

0, 0

2020 — Our Reckoning
We have been to hell
and back, it was gruelling and
relentless for us.

Have our lives been changed
in ways we could never have
imagined, as we

are opening up?
Theatres will once again host
performances and

we will hear music,
see friends, family, socialise,
in COVID-safe ways.

The premiers did the
heavy lifting to control
the virus against

criticism from
Fed. pollies who coat-tailed on
the states' unsung work

but at least here in
our hospitals doctors did
not have to decide

which patients got a
life-saving ventilator
or who lived or died.

Meanwhile Europe and
UK wrestle with shocking
second wave outbreaks

while the US has
given up trying to curb
the virus at all.

They are hoping that
a vaccine will come soon to
tame the pandemic,

while Trump grandstands and
seeks injunctions in the courts,
incites rebellion.

And in a rage, he
is pardoning his crooked,
jailbird cronies while

he's executing
prisoners on death-row, his last
act of bastardry

before he leaves the
White House. But in a strange twist,
Trumpism became

Trumpianity,
the new pseudo-religion
of the USA.

But this God doesn't
care about the hundreds of
thousands of people

who are contracting
the virus, dying in droves,
their bodies stored in

refrigerator
trucks because funeral parlours
have run out of space.

2020 has
been a year of pain—bushfires,
drought, floods, recession

and killer virus.
And Black Lives Matter showed us
how racism is

all pervasive in
our communities, in each
of us, in our souls.

Will we be different
after our upside-down lives?
How will we look back

on this year of our
reckoning when we lost all
sense of control in

our fragile little
lives? We had to dive into
our souls to survive

a plague and all those
world-wide events that shaped our
year as memorable.

It was the worst of
times but also the best, where
we were forced to look

into a mirror
to see ourselves like never
before and take stock,

all the while knowing
that behind every cranny
lurks this deadly plague.

Epilogue (or so I thought ...)

Counting off the Days

Nine months gone and I
look back and see no markers
to say time has passed.

My empty diary
symbolised the yawning days,
time passing slowly.

Like another age
our lives fell into the black,
arhythmical hole.

I ask myself: *what
have I done in these strange times?*
How have I kept my

sanity when the
centre wasn't holding firm?
I don't know. I have

no pot holders, felt
hats, quilt rugs or sourdough
bread to show, and no

grand projects done, just
these humble haikus that tell
the tale of how we

lived through this virus
in existential despair
counting off the days.

Snap Lockdown 4.0

in Victoria

Called by Acting Premier James Merlino
on 27 May 2021

Day 1 – 28 May

Announcement
Not just Melbourne, but
whole state locked down in *circuit
breaker* we needed.

Déjà vu
We've been here before,
we thought we'd outgunned you pest,
beaten you into

submission with our
heavy duty lockdowns, our
no-nonsense approach

you were virtually
gone from our lives, so we thought,
big pain in the arse

it was going so
well. I was back doing my
'normal things'. Life was

in full swing—music,
hockey, discussion group, talks,
not wearing a mask,

now you're having the
last laugh as we go back in
to a snap lockdown.

You surfaced like a
floating turd. We should have been
better prepared but

our complacency
ruined us, causing vaccine
hesitancy. Now

we count the cost of
our foolishness as we are
prisoners once again.

Bickering
Governments bicker:
who's responsible for this
dire situation?

Who did what or who
didn't do what they should have?
I don't give a rats.

Familiar Territory
We've done this before,
so, while we're angry, anxious,
frustrated, we know

what to do, how to
navigate a lockdown and
keep our sanity.

We go back to our
COVID routines, strategies
that worked well for us,

we're old hands now so
break out the COVID cuisine
menu, get a book

crack the Diet Coke,
huddle in front of the fire,
hunker down for now.

Business Limbo
Businesses are in
limbo with no JobKeeper
to support them and

are hoping for a
package from State Government.
So far Feds have done

nothing to support
them. Cooperation is
desperately needed.

Day 2 – 29 May

Case Numbers
No huge breakout in
case numbers is a relief
but testing times still.

Feds Abandon Us
Federal government
declines to offer Vic. some
financial support.

Responsible
Feds responsible
for vaccine roll out and yes,
hotel quarantine

both of which have failed
miserably. They're shambolic
and disorganised.

Flocking
Thousands are flocking
to vaccination centres.
Suddenly there is

some urgency from
those who were hesitant to
be vaccinated.

It takes a crisis
to motivate people who
are now running scared.

Close Contacts
*There are thousands and
thousands of close contacts that
still have to go through*

*the incubation
period who could become
symptomatic*, warns

Prof. Sutton as we
wait out the time to see how
the virus will run.

Exposure Sites
The number of the
exposure sites keeps growing—
now into hundreds!

Circus Needed Again
Footy again is
our distraction while we are
confined to our homes

at least the Dees are
giving me some joy with a
top of the table

victory over the
Western Bulldogs. Now they are
favourites to win flag.

I'm not convinced yet,
too many years of Demons'
let-down and heartbreak.

Day 3 – 30 May

Steady as We Go
Some relief with no
escalation of cases
says report today.

Deadly New Strain
Very dangerous
new strain has been uncovered
in Vietnam which

is a combo of
the so-called Indian and
UK mutations

and this hybrid is
faster-spreading and is much
more transmissible

at a rate not known
or seen before. We need to
be prepared for this.

Dan Tehan Insult
State asks Feds for some
support after announcing
a rescue package

for small businesses.
They ask the Feds to match it,
they're still holding out

*Out of work Vics should
go to Centrelink to see
if they qualify*

for support from the
government—says Dan Tehan.
Unbelievable.

What an insult to
Vic. workers who are not to
blame for loss of jobs.

Will Dan Tehan be
going to Centrelink if
he loses his seat?

Once again party
politics rears its ugly,
vile, self-serving head.

If it was Gladys
asking for help, I wonder,
would Feds refuse her?

*I am angry and
disappointed* says Pallas.
We are forgotten

by Feds who don't seem
to care, saying it was *our
choice* to lockdown state.

South Australia Leak
Quarantine leak came
from SA but no bagging
them from mate ScoMo.

If it had come from
Vic. imagine the hoo-ha
from the Lib. shit heads

and yet we are now
being punished once again
for what's happening.

Aged Care Again
The virus outbreak
has spread to aged care as a
worker's positive

test result throws the
home into lockdown. We hope
no one dies from this.

Wake-Up Call
This COVID outbreak's
a vaccination wake-up
call but who'll heed it?

Scuffle and Shuffle
So, several dozen
anti-lockdown protestors
clashed with police at

the Flagstaff Gardens,
while others queued to have tests
or vaccinations.

Day 4 – 31 May

Feels Longer
It feels longer than
four days as time seems to be
in the strangest warp.

Self-Congratulations
The Libs' conference in
Canberra, where they patted their
backs in festive style

viewed from our lockdown-
city, looked self-serving and
full of arrogance,

no apology
between backslaps and worship
of Menzies and no

offer to help us.
Morrison had three jobs in
this pandemic, yep,

quarantine, money,
and vaccinations. He ducked
out of the first, stopped

the second too soon
and messed up the third big time.
Sheer incompetence.

Their cold-heartedness
and lack of empathy is
mind-blowingly cruel.

Surprise Efficiency
The Prince of Shambles
Boris Johnson is at least
getting vaccines done.

Aged Care Worry
Another worker
and resident in aged care
home test positive.

The worker had had
one shot of a vaccine but
clearly, we need two.

If they don't get on
top of it, I can see it
rampaging through aged-

care homes, with deaths to
come. Who knows? Who cares for these
old and vulnerable?

In the Balance
End to Vic. lockdown
hangs in the balance as the
infections climb up.

Extend Lockdown
Experts are saying
extend lockdown another
week to ensure that

all the possible
cases are flushed out in the
incubation time.

Neck and Neck
Prof. Sutton says: *we're
neck and neck with the virus,
an absolute beast.*

Day 5 – 1 June

Going Badly
It's not going well
and an extension of the
lockdown looks likely.

Restless
I am beginning
to feel restless and on edge,
my unquiet mind

is lurching into
a dark place as we feel the
isolation grab.

It's a bit different,
this time, more depressing and
soul-crushingly grim.

Our taste of freedom
whetted our appetites for
a more normal life

but here we are, back
to our hapless prison lives
like 12 months ago.

I don't know what to
think or feel. It is so weird
and so incomplete.

Ring of Steel
Talk of *Ring of Steel*
again, to cut off Melbourne
from Regional Vic.

Mental Health Dive
People's mental health
taking a dive as they call
crisis lines for help.

We Learnt Nothing
Have we learnt nothing
from last year? As aged-care staff
are still working at

different sites and are
exposing residents to
the virus—again.

Age Care Minister
Colbeck could not give
answers to the senators
as to how many

workers in aged care
had had vaccines. The shambles
is just breathtaking.

Vic. government steps
in and is now having a
vaccine blitz for them.

12 Months Ago
we were scrambling in
a world that had flipped into
insanity and

I was captured by
Master Chef and by Poh's fate,
it entertained me

helped me to survive,
now I don't seem to care. I
watch other things like

the shows on Netflix—
WWII docos are my
current absorption.

Day 6 – 2 June

Surprise, Surprise
Poorer countries don't
have access to vaccines. Why
am I not surprised?

Typhoid Mary
So, if we are not
careful with aged care, we will
have Typhoid Mary

as charge-nurse running
the show and wreaking havoc
on old sitting ducks.

So Many
There are so many
different strains of the virus,
it's a moving feast.

Popping Up
Virus is popping
up in other states raising
fears of it spreading.

COVID Commander in Chief
The COVID testing
Commander is one Jeroen-
no-nonsense-Weimar.

Jeroen Weimar says
the State is grappling
with *what is likely to be
the fastest-moving*

*outbreak yet to hit
Australia*. With *stranger to
stranger* transmission,

and as exposure
sites increase in number, we're
more and more on edge.

Acting Premier
Merlino's running
the state while Dan is resting
under the doona.

Comfort Food
Stocked up on ice-cream,
Toblerone chocolate, in case
of longer lockdown.

Warning about New Strain
*If strain continues
unchecked, people will die*, says
Professor Sutton.

11.30 a.m.
The rumblings about
the lockdown extension are
growing. I await.

12 noon Lockdown Continues
Shit, bugger, bum, poop,
pubic hair, more pain, as we
are kept in lockdown.

More Deadly
New variant of
the virus more contagious,
more deadly so *we*

*have to run it to
the ground*. And eradicate
it out of our lives.

Journos' Interrogation
Angry journos grill
Prof. Sutton about reasons
for this extension.

Cut Off
Melbourne cut off from
regional Victoria—
virtual ring of steel.

Police to do spot
checks along the roads rather
than having checkpoints.

Why Melbourne?
Why do we have these
virus outbreaks? Bad luck? Bad
management? Why us?

Our fourth lockdown in
16 months adding to our
collective anger.

We're called the *lockdown
capital*. Is it cultural,
geographical?

Melbourne Uni dons
say: *COVID's random* and it's
more likely bad luck.

Humour Lacking
My sense of humour
has died. I cannot see the
funny side of things.

Cancelled
Our lives have been on
hold and now everything's been
cancelled or postponed—

arts projects, theatre
performances, music gigs,
our lives are empty.

Lifeline
I'm dialling up a
haiku to help me get through
this challenging time.

The haiku can give
me some therapy and much
needed life support.

Fobbing Us Off
If Josh keeps fobbing
off Merlino's plea for help,
Libs may lose votes in

Victoria. Watch
this space. We're not amused; the
ballot box may speak.

Day 7 – 3 June

Disputed Evidence
Now there is contrary
epidemiology
from Prof. McCaw that

disputes Prof. Sutton's
claim that the *fast-moving beast*
is more infectious.

McCaw thinks that such
doomsday language is not that
helpful and will seed

alarm in people's
minds. So, is the *Kappa* strain
more contagious than

the previous strains?
Who to believe? We're at the
mercy of experts.

11.30 a.m. Fed. Assistance
A decision is
imminent from Feds about
assistance for Vic.

Frydenberg
*still finds it baffling
that kids can't go to school* and
regions *are locked down.*

Quarantine Facility
Avalon in box-
seat to house Victoria's
new quarantine place.

Things To Do
A play's the thing, sweet
music, dance away heartache,
art for art's sake, there

are books to read, there's
solace in celluloid or
pat a cat and dog.

Record High
Vaccinations hit
a record high as people
scramble to get one.

QR Codes
QR Codes to get
into supermarkets, shops.
They're now mandatory.

Will I need one to
get into heaven or hell,
or my own lounge room?

Circus Imperative
Footy players are
given dispensation to
travel interstate

to play games. Canny
move by governments to keep
us placated by

keeping the footy
circus going. Following
our teams is one big

diversion where we
lose ourselves in the drama
and theatre of it.

2 p.m. Morrison Dragged
kicking and screaming
to finally provide some
financial aid to

Victorians but
conditions apply such as
they must have used up

all pandemic sick
leave and must have less than ten
thousand dollars in

their liquid assets,
nor can they be receiving
any other funds.

States are to support
business and Feds to provide
households with support.

Open for Business
Regional Vic. will
open tonight with freedom
of movement for them.

COVID Shopping
Masked faces, no smiles,
after we've QR coded
in. We sign papers

with an unused pen
which we then place in the used
pen jar after use.

Day 8 – 4 June

Empathy?
Is there empathy
for Melburnians from the
rest of Australia?

Questions
Lockdown extension
faces scrutiny over
false 'stranger' spread fear.

Remember
Hey, remember the
COVIDSafe App? Eight million
dollar useless dud?

It's still costing us,
75,000 bucks
every month to run.

PM's Overrule
PM to lobby
States and Territories to
force aged care workers

to get the vaccine.
His advisory group said
not to make it a

compulsory thing.
Union boss says: *This is not
Communist China,*

government has *not
advertised the vaccines in
a positive way.*

Millennials
have a new craze, they
want something they can't get—
a vaccination.

Seeing young people
overseas get it frustrates
them with slow rollout.

Experts have pushed for
an open rollout for all
who want a vaccine.

Is there enough in
our vaccine stock to do this?
We need more Pfizer.

EOFY Sales
Retail giants gear
up for massive discounts post
pandemic sales loss.

The Variants
Alpha, Beta and
Gamma, Delta, Epsilon,
Zeta, Iota,

Theta, Eta and
Kappa—various names. They
are all Greek to me!

Will an Omega
strain of the virus be the
one that wipes us out?

Waleed Aly Writes
Blame-shifting and scare-
mongering as well as folks
playing fast and loose

with the facts helps no
one during a pandemic.
Could not agree more.

Waleed Also Says: The Ordinary
parry and thrust of
political life doesn't
serve us well, as it

allows lame, lazy
narratives to thrive. I think
he's on to something.

By Next Week
we will have endured
170
days in hard lockdown.

Day 9 – 5 June

Race to Trace
Plea for a 'global
effort' on the super-fast
Delta strain in Vic.

Risks Too Great
Risk of outbreak too
great. PM urged to ditch the
hotel quarantine.

Go Dees!
Dees outplay Lions
and are premiership favourites—
one week at a time.

Hopes Dashed
New Delta outbreak
dashes hope of a lockdown
reprieve for Melbourne.

Two Variants
Melbourne now has two
clusters with the Kappa strain
and the Delta strain.

More Transmissible
Delta variant
of COVID-19 now in
Melbourne may be more

transmissible than
the other variants of
the virus yet seen.

Afterthought
Aged-care staff are a
vaccination afterthought
in this shemozzle

of a rollout for
which Hunt was responsible.
At the same time, Feds

scrapped support payments
designed to stop staff working
at multiple sites.

Spin Doctor
The only thing that
Morrison's on top of is
political spin.

Yep, our *Scotty from
Marketing* knows how to make
us believe his lies.

Ghost Towns
CBDs taking
a hit with people working
from comfort of home.

What's their Agenda?
Anti-vaxxers plan
to harass people who are
standing in queues to

get vaccinated.
What do they want to achieve?
It bemuses me.

Day 10 – 6 June

No Hockey
Another weekend
passes without hockey—the
season's flying by.

QAnon and the PM
PM's close friend is
a QAnon follower—
an ABC *Four*

*Corner*s show asks: Is
PM a security
risk? The show is pulled.

Feud
Barely a day goes
by without the Libs feuding
with the ABC.

A Matter of Time
More COVID outbreaks
only a matter of time
if slow rollout of

vaccines continue.
Public needs to know when we
have enough vaccines.

Army Brought In
PM has brought in
army to boost the troubled
rollout, appointing

Lieutenant General
John Frewen to oversee
the vaccine programme.

Comfort Culture
I need some comfort
culture to binge on to cheer
up my dragging days.

COVID War Rooms
Contact tracing war
rooms are military-inspired
mission commands where

the plan is to: go
fast, stop COVID, report back
to base. It's working

giving Vics a good
level of protection from
the COVID virus.

Dedicated folks—
our contact tracers-working
to keep us all safe.

Mental Murder
Psychological
struggles, doom-scrolling of the
Net and the impact

of latest lockdown
has a hopelessness attached
to uncertainty.

Pandemically Prosperous
Some people live pay
day to pay day while others
are raking it in!

The ASX has
hit record highs, real estate
booms while luxury

and sports car sales are
thriving. Economic growth
exceeds predictions.

Our weakest link is
rank complacency by the
populace and worse

our political
leaders to make sure we're all
vaccinated and

future-proofed against
the virus that's impoverished
some, enriched others.

Lost Art of Survival
Victorians have
struggled to regain some of
the techniques they used

to get them through the
2020 lockdowns and
are battling with their

compounding distress,
emotional fatigue and
virus exhaustion.

Soaring Jobless
Applications for
the dole have soared as many
struggle to pay rent.

Dark Cloud
of anxiety
hangs over small business who
battle to survive.

Where They're At
ScoMo is walking
on sunshine, Labor is sleep-
walking off a cliff.

Inward
Deeper in my own
head, inward dwelling rather
than looking outside,

dealing with my own
demons, somehow this time round
the external fades.

Day 11 – 7 June

Lessons
What's the pandemic
taught us about ourselves? That
social discipline's

in our DNA?
That some are more equal than
others? That trust in

government has climbed?
While mistakes are made, we are
happy to oblige?

I awake to the
mental stress of the lockdown,
confined to home and

reading that kids are
suffering with their fenced-in,
no-friends lives. They have

replaced the old as
our most vulnerable. With their
learning now online

can technology
deliver a meaningful
educational

experience or
is that a delusion pushed
by the bureaucrats?

Teachers are fed up,
we are all fed up but do
we trust our leaders

that this lockdown is
about community first,
not their approval?

We live day to day
in an information surge—
journalists write their

op. eds while pollies
hit the media—info
overload for us.

Our faith is tested.
Are we being hoodwinked or
are our eyes wide shut?

I can't help but feel
that if Melburnians are
not broken yet then

we soon will be as
each day passes in our sad,
unquiet city.

Exposure Numbers
Exposure sites near
400 as concerns grow
for the Delta strain.

Racing Against the Clock
Two crucial days to
determine Melbourne's lockdown
plans despite setbacks.

'No Snapback' CHO Warns
no large gatherings
or a full MCG—it's
a day-by-day thing

we may face weeks of
some restrictions even as
lockdown is lifted.

Heart v Head
My heart yearns for its
freedom, my head says lockdown
is necessary.

Day 12 – 8 June

When?
When will it be done
and dusted, over with, gone,
consigned to dustbin?

ScoMo Pressure
ScoMo says: *End it
ASAP,* citing New
South Wales yet again

as the Gold Standard
for localised lockdowns—but
Melbourne is unique

says Prof. Sutton, as
the virus is spreading too
quickly and sites of

exposure are not
confined to small areas—
we need this lockdown.

Cluster
Growing West Melbourne
cluster infected with the
Delta strain concerns.

School Cases
Concerns over the
cluster of cases at North
Melbourne Primary School

which is closed, students,
teachers infected, families
in isolation.

Patience Wearing
My reservoir of
patience is stretched and wearing
thin. I must hold on.

Source Found
Source of Delta strain
pinpointed by tracers—it's
a welcome breakthrough.

A traveller from Sri
Lanka in quarantine had
tested positive,

how he infected
families linked to the primary
school is a mystery.

RUOK?
People ask me: How
are you coping with lockdown?
I wish I could say

great! But I feel like
COVID shit. Groundhog Day won't
let the future dawn

without caveats
of 'you can't do this or that.'
The walls of my mind

surround me with a
deep foreboding. I ask: When
will these plague days end?

Routine Blip
I don't have the same
sanity-making routine
as I had last year.

Cabin fever strikes,
just want to fledge my clipped wings,
fly skyward and breathe.

Dan Conspiracy
State Libs are pushing
conspiracies about Dan's
injuries. They ask

stupid questions and
dispute him being paid while
on sick leave, claiming

a nefarious
cover up by Labor and
Dan to hoodwink us.

Are Libs that desperate
that they stoop to idiot
tactics and fictions?

Day 13 – 9 June

9.30 a.m. Tell Us
We just want to know
our fate. Tell us what is to
happen to us now?

We got it last year
when cases were hundreds and
people were dying

but now with so few
we are frustrated, angry
and bemused by it.

11.30 a.m. Merlino says:
This is a good day.
Is it? I can only go
25ks, and

can't have visitors,
nor can I play music with
my local trio.

I can see people
being pissed off, rebellious
disobedient.

Government's hell bent
on getting to zero case
numbers come what may.

Prof. Sutton says there's
*really no alternative,
no grumbling along*

*with one or two of
these cases. It started with
one case in Wollert.*

I want my freedom
but am trying to see the
bigger picture here.

Urgent
investigations
in three States as Vic. traveller
defies Vic's lockdown.

The Super Storm

On the night of 9 June a super storm hit the outer east and northern parts of Melbourne as well as Gippsland. There was significant flooding in Traralgon and Sale. The Dandenong and Macedon Ranges sustained a lot of damage with trees down across roads and over houses and powerlines down. The Yarra River flooded at Yarra Glen with the road to Lilydale cut off. Extensive power outages occurred with thousands of homes and businesses left in the dark. Not only were we dealing with the COVID restrictions but now we had to live with the aftermath of the storm's damage and life without electricity.

Day 14 – 10 June

Day 1 Without Power

Super Storm
Super storm lashes
Melbourne—wind, rain, trees down and
power outages,

the pandemic flies
away for the while as we
all count the storm's cost.

Into the Dark
What else can go wrong?
Home in darkness, no power,
internet or phones,

communication
impossible, no idea
what is happening

in the world away
from our epicentre. As
for the virus, what?

I Just Heard There
are four new cases
all in one family, so
it bubbles away

in the background like
a thief stealing away our
lives without justice.

Bunker Down
So, bunker down and
prepare for a candlelight
dinner, early bed.

Second Death
Calm is urged by the
regulator after a
second death linked to

AstraZeneca
vaccine is revealed—this may
put the wind up folks.

Conspiracies
Dan Conspiracies
running on steroids with wild,
mad accusations.

Day 15 – 11 June

Day 2 Without Power

Forward Movement?
No new locally
acquired cases—are we
now moving forward?

Surge
Surge in mental health
distress as people struggle
with their emotions.

An increase in those
calling helplines and seeking
mental health support.

What Next?
Bloody COVID and
now we're sitting in the dark
wondering: what next?

Making do with what
we have—batteries, chargers
and our camping gear.

Inequality
The vaccination
inequality around
the world is so stark.

One billion doses
of vaccine to be promised
to poorer countries.

Offline Irony
Supermarket cash
registers go offline—cash
transactions only!

Pandemic sent us
to a cashless world—money
was filthy lucre.

Cash is the only
way now to buy essentials
at local traders.

Bank had to close and
there are no ATMs so
we cannot get cash.

These floods and power
failures have exposed the flaws
of the techno world.

The Cause
COVID and super
storm almost certainly caused
by Dan and 5G!

Day 16 – 12 June

Day 3 Without Power

Tested
Plague, flood and blackout,
we are being tested for
our resilience.

We can't take much more.
All we need now is a plague
of locusts to come!

Mystery
Mystery cases in the
city puts people on edge—
we're on tenterhooks.

Dickheads
Recalcitrant Vics
nabbed at border attempting
to cross interstate.

Kind Friends
Shower and breakfast
with kind friends who offer us
much needed support.

Three Days On
No power now for
three days—generators still
whirring in background.

Tried and True
No computer so
these haikus are written with
yes, pen and paper.

Doubts
Doubts over mask and
travel rules, says expert—so
what are we to think?

Politics of Vaccinations
Vaccine donations
to countries in our region—
is it politics

so we can say we
are better than the Chinese
and more generous?

CBD Dead
The city is dead
empty offices leave a
hole in CBD,

cafés, hotels and
small businesses struggle for
trade—sad, empty streets.

Melbourne no longer
the most liveable city—
it's unliveable.

The Hills Are Alive with
the happy hum of
generators as we all
keep our fridges and

freezers, all laden
with food and drink, alive and
to keep our lights on.

7.15 p.m. Power Company Posts
power to be out
for another seven days!
Feels like I am in

Gilead and Aunt
Lydia is about to
darken my doorstep!

Killing Time
The day is spent with
books, writing and radio
until night descends.

Pitching In
Crisis mode—lots of
offers of generators,
showers, food, support

from local members
of CFA—it really
is a family.

Darkened Mind
My mind plays with the
dark side, granting my demons
too much room to move.

Day 17 – 13 June

1.30 a.m. And Then There Was Light!
Miracle, power
back on! And now back to our
COVID abnormal.

For Granted
Assessing what we
took for granted after shock
of no power source.

Packed Up
Everything packed up—
cords, generators, chargers,
lights, torches—all gone.

House back to normal
and life back to its daily
pandemic routine.

So Good
It's so good to have
all our technology back
and normality.

The Lightness of Being
How different the world
looks today, with our lives now
basking in the light.

My mood has lifted,
my voices are quieter,
my demons are stilled.

Testing Plummets
Branches of virus
infections may be going
undetected as

testing rates plummet
by half in Victoria—
concern for huge drop.

Government Threat
*If you do not get
tested, we won't open up.*
I do not like threats.

Day 18 – 14 June

G7 Meeting
Australia exposed
for vaccination failings
at G7 and

PM is forced to
defend our slow rollout to
other world leaders.

Brave
It would be a brave
government to keep us in
lockdown past this week.

Limbo
Holiday plans in
limbo with uncertainty
on the restrictions.

Melbourne v The Burbs
Melbourne's CBD
has been hammered, people are
working from home and

shopping online and
a wariness of public
transport that has kept

folks away who had
made it the engine room of
state's economy.

The pandemic has
injected new life into
the long neglected

suburban shopping
strips, backstreets and parks to make
what some leaders have

promised, but not done—
a *city of villages,*
the *20-minute*

neighbourhood where folks
buy local, work local, live
local, play local.

Localism is
a threat to the CBD
which the government

has invested in
with development projects.
They're in the hot seat

now that crowds have gone.
Cranes have thinned on the skyline
shopfronts are vacant,

abandoned building
projects leave scars like bomb sites.
Government scrambles

propping up Melbourne
by purchasing apartments
for social housing

and encouraging
students and public servants
back to the centre.

The rhythm of the
city has changed, it's gone back
four decades in time.

A battle ensues
for the heart of Melbourne. Will
the suburbs win or

will the city find
its mojo again and lure
the missing crowds back?

Day 19 – 15 June

9 a.m. Today
No new cases but
source of Delta outbreak may
remain a mystery.

Still No Power
Homes are still in the
dark after super storm with
a long wait ahead.

Old Vaccine Hope
100-year-old
TB vaccine offers some
hope against virus.

Losing Track
Losing track of the
days when not much is on—what
day is it again?

16 Long Months
It's been 16 months
of life with COVID for we
Melburnians. We

endured those endless
lockdowns, life interrupted,
when everything was

turned on its head and
we were house-bound, suburb-bound
life-bound, rebuffed by

our compatriots
who shut us out. We were the
unclean contagion.

We peer into each
other's eyes with a knowing
look. Melburnians

understand. Yes, we
all went through hell as we sat
alone in our homes,

jobless, poverty
at our doors, restless in the
curfew, our lives in

free-fall, spiralling
into the COVID vortex,
wondering: Why? We

kept our distance, wore
our masks, counted the days, watched
Dan's press conferences,

waited and waited
for the virus to be tamed,
braved the set-backs and

the grinding, ceaseless,
Groundhog Days of thinking that
this will never end.

Melburnians will
always have a deep bond with
each other when words

won't be needed to
say: *yes, I was there. I lived
through the cruellest times*

*with you, when we bore
the brunt of the fight on our
pandemic island.*

3.30 p.m. Breaking News
An apartment block
sent into lockdown after
surprise COVID spread,

two new cases which
were locally acquired
discovered today.

Day 20 – 16 June

9 a.m. In the Dark
We're in the dark. Just
tell us what's happening and
when we will be free!

Impatient
So, I find myself
becoming impatient with
the pandemic rules.

I'm over it. We're
all over it, while trying
to see big picture.

12 noon
More cases, dozens
more exposure sites, as rule
decision looms large.

Market Site Exposure
South Melbourne Market
visited by a person
who was positive.

12.15 p.m. Merlino Speaks
Some relief for us—
25 kilometre
rule scrapped and we can

have two visitors
in our homes. Yay, finally
my trio can meet.

Some normality
is back in our lives. We can
move more freely and

play sport, make music
and travel to the regions—
it's a beginning.

COVID Snow
People going to
the snow have to be tested
before they get there.

The Future
All we know is that
the future is uncertain.
Who knows when the next

lockdown will occur?
When the next batch of cases
will throw a spanner

into our lives yet
again? We live with this odd
reality that

our lives are not our
own, that at any time they
can be upturned by

this odious thing,
that we are enslaved to a
pandemic monster

who can turn our homes
into prisons, and our streets
into dangerous

super spreader ways,
where we look at people with
some suspicion, as

everyone is a
threat and no one's safe because
this is not over.

Dan Told He
*must resign to give
us a fresh start,* by Kennett,
Bolt and co. Really?

Kept My Sanity
I am still sane in
spite of all the obstacles
the latest dramas

presented to me.
Yes, I prevailed over my
mind's vast madding crowd.

Snap Lockdown 5.0

Premier Daniel Andrews Announces
Another Lockdown on 15 July

Lockdown Announced — 15 July

Back On Job
Poor Dan, not long back
on the job and he has to
put us in lockdown.

Birthday Gift
Happy birthday gift.
Liberty City no more.
Five day lockdown called.

Dan Says
We have got no choice,
we have got to do this, go
hard and go fast. And

we only get one
chance to stop it so we're not
locked up for five months.

Fatigue
Number five—we are
weary of lockdowns—God, how
much more can we take?

Melburnians have
now endured over six long
months of hard lockdowns.

It Started with
two removalists
super spreading the virus
through South Australia,

New South Wales and in
Victoria, were maskless,
and now we're pickled!

Circuit Breaker
Another circuit
breaker needed to stop the
Delta variant

which has been the game-
changer because it is so
bloody contagious.

Trouble Brewing
New South Wales under
pressure as case numbers start
to accelerate.

NSW v Victoria
Two States, two different
ways to manage the virus—
who wins bragging rights?

Gold Standard State has
lost its lustre and yes, it
was only Fool's Gold.

The Lonely Lockdown
First lockdown alone.
Not sure how I'll deal with the
loneliness this time.

Back on Haikus
What else is there to
do? I'm back on the haikus
they are my saviours.

Day 1 — 16 July

Schadenfreude Karma
It must have been my
perverse pleasure in watching
Gladys' dramas

and the Gold Standard
State not so golden that has
brought on *our* lockdown.

The Great Divides
Us and them divide
could be long-term legacy
of the pandemic.

States versus the Feds,
employed versus unemployed,
rule flouters versus

those who follow rules,
office workers versus those
working from their homes,

the vaccinated
versus those who can't get one,
hotel quarantined

who are paying for
it versus those able to
isolate at home,

those who made it home
before borders were slammed shut
to rest of the world,

students who can go
to school versus those who are
learning remotely.

Will we recover
from the things that divide us
now more than ever?

Raising Dashing
Accumulated
grief—hopes raised, hopes dashed, hopes raised,
hopes dashed, despair, hope?

Day 2 — 17 July

Settling In
Settling into the
humdrum sameness of lockdown
mindfulness practice.

Sydney Braces
Sydney braces for
tougher lockdown after a
long cabinet meeting.

Maybe Gladys is
getting spooked by the surge in
virus case numbers?

Dan on the Delta Variant
*We can't be running
alongside this thing. We have
to be out in front.*

Wellbeing
The resilience
of people has ebbed and flowed
there is increased stress.

Outpacing
Delta variant's
outpacing contact tracers,
next four months crucial.

National Strategy
Calls from experts for
a national strategy
to eliminate
rather than suppress
the Delta strain from all states
and territories.

Dobbers?
Has the pandemic
turned us into a nation
who rats on neighbours?

Gen C
Young kids are growing
up in COVID lockdown world
So, how will they fare?

The Times
Philosophical
times, we ask: what do we owe
each other when the

haves and have nots are
not evenly bearing the
brunt of pandemic?

We need our poets
and artists to make sense of
the virus zeitgeist,

to tell the stories,
create a vision we can
share with each other.

Day 3 — 18 July

Alone
Contemplating my
aloneness—no one to talk
with, sit with, eat with,

laugh with, cry with, share
my frustrations—solitude
is shared with three cats.

Scrutiny Showtime
Leaders are under
scrutiny more than ever
and we judge how they

perform, we hang on
every word, pressers outrate
everything, they are

actors in soapies
and politics is showbiz
and their performance

gives us glimpse in
to their souls—it's showtime now,
scene one, and action!

So ScoMo will be
working on his smirk, Gladys
trying to define

essential, and Dan
pretending not to sound like
he's over-rehearsed

or criticising
ScoMo when he really is.
Scene two, and action!

Anti-Vaxxer Capital
Mullumbimby folks
equate anti-maskers to
freedom fighters and

No Mask, We Don't Ask!
signs are in shop windows, they're
anti-government

and flouting COVID
regulations, accosting
people who wear masks.

Has mixed messaging
from ScoMo muddied things to
create this problem?

Day 4 — 19 July

No Freedom Yet
It simply cannot
end, says Dan with worrying
spread of the virus.

I know this is not
the news people want to hear.
We wait patiently.

Melbourne's Lord Mayor ...
calls for jab targets
so we can open up and
live with the virus.

Olympics
Australian athletes
face virus scare, as foreign
athletes positive.

Winter Lockdown
I need something to
lift me out of these tiresome
winter COVID blues.

UK Freedom Day
Brits to be freed from
their restrictions today. So,
cautious or reckless?

Day 5 — 20 July

Traced Back
It began with the
MCC Members' Reserve
and the rugby at

AAMI Park—all were
super-spreader events that
infected many

who took virus to
Regional Victoria
as tentacles spread.

11.30 a.m. Extension
Blow, Dan extends the
lockdown for another week.
We need more time and

*We can't run the risk
that there are cases out there
we don't know about,*

Mother Dies
The super-spreader
removalists' mother dies
infected by them.

Another Lockdown State
South Australia goes
into lockdown following
case numbers climbing.

Stabilising?
Gladys says: *We have
stabilised the virus,* asks
folks to do right thing.

Ennui
Lockdown ennui is
starting to take hold and
things look bleak and grim.

Olympics
The lonely games with
no crowds to cheer athletes on,
no buzz for winners

and sadly athletes
are to present themselves with
their shiny medals.

Vigilance
Mental health watch is
imperative as lockdowns
are a fact of life.

National Crisis
13 million are
in lockdown across our land
as Delta strain spreads.

Day 6 — 21 July

Hard Border
Hard border between
Victoria and New South
Wales reinstated.

Victorians north
of border cannot return
home from today. Blow.

Global Time Bomb
Will the Olympics
be a global time bomb with
athletes spreading bug?

Prof. Sutton's World of Hurt
*We would be in a
world of hurt if we hadn't
done what we have done*

*and there would have been
thousands of cases without
this current lockdown.*

Plaudits
Plaudits galore are
being thrown at Gladys by
ScoMo and his mates.

She has done a great
job in managing virus
according to them.

Federal government
bent over backwards to help
out Gladys which riled

many of us in
Victoria who felt she
was The Chosen One.

Longer
Surprise, the lockdown
has gone longer than the five
days they said it would.

There is no snap back
to the seemingly normal
life we had before,

only an easing
of restrictions to keep us
calm and compliant.

Day 7 — 22 July

Lockdown Turnaround
Now Michael O'Brien
is saying Dan should have had
stricter borders and

then called for quicker
lockdowns. It's a departure
from his previous

stance where he has been
outspoken about knee-jerk
public health measures

from Dan's government.
Liberal frontbencher Matthew
Guy questioned hard state

borders, asking: *Are
we colonies or are we
a country?* So, with

over 100
cases in nine days, his words
didn't age so well.

The State Liberals are
in a political mess
seeking relevance.

NSW Dramas
Virus taking hold.
Gladys is *expecting case
numbers to go up.*

Says, *we need to brace
ourselves for that and it does
mean more hospital*

*presentations. It
is cruel how contagious this
virus is.* Too true.

Gone
My schadenfreude
has well and truly gone as
hard times come again.

Even feeling some
lockdown solidarity
with Sydneysiders.

Meanwhile
Victoria is
battling to control the spread
of the Delta strain.

Get Vaccinated
PM is urging
Queenslanders to get their jab,
not to wait and see.

Loneliness Check
Thought I'd struggle more
being by myself—surprise,
I'm OK with me

even though the days
are long and nights are longer
solitude is fine.

Day 8 — 23 July

Gladys' Trouble
Infected workers.
Byron Bay virus alarm,
and more bad numbers.

NSW
Gladys calling it
national emergency
Sydney cases soar.

She's now pushing to
broaden vaccine roll out to
get first vaccines done

in virus-hit south-
western and western Sydney
and young people too.

Vaccine Rollout Apology
Apology from
ScoMo for tardy rollout.
Says *it's back on track.*

Double Standards
Appalled at double
standards—sports teams train and film
shoots happen while arts

companies cannot
rehearse a show—the lack of
support breathtaking.

New Ring
Dan calls for a *Ring
of Steel* around Sydney, a
bit cheeky by Dan.

While *trend is with us
for rules to ease*. Is Dan now
being mischievous?

The L Word
Gladys had trouble
using the L word—could not
say Lockdown, it's too

political and
sounds like Victoria and
our man Dan Andrews.

Day 9 — 24 July

Olympics Opening
No crowd, few athletes,
Naomi Osaka lights
flame for sombre games

while outside there are
people protesting who do
not want Olympics

and already there
have been 11 athletes
who've caught the virus!

Checkpoint Charlie
Travellers from the north
will have to get through Checkpoint
Charlie at border.

Dreaming
We dream of getting
away to places where we
can forget lockdowns.

Compare the Pair
Is Liberal lockdown
better than Labor lockdown?
Gladys versus Dan.

Protests
Thousands of people
in Sydney, Melbourne, Brisbane
take to the streets to

protest the against the
lockdowns, waving flags, crying
Wake Up Australia!

Day 10 — 25 July

NSW Protests
Super spreader fears
as detectives hunt anti-
lockdown protestors.

Melbourne's Rally
Dan *can't rule out an
extension to restrictions
if cases come out*

*of the protests on
Saturday,* calling anti-
lockdowners *selfish.*

*It puts all the work
everyone has done at risk.
They're self-indulgent.*

*We can't vaccinate
against selfishness. They are
putting lives at risk.*

Vaccine Politics
Pressure on states to
share their portion of Pfizer
drugs with New South Wales.

Dan says no to New
South Wales request after they
indicated last

year they wouldn't help
Vic. with vaccines. Is this tit-
for-tat politics?

JobKeeper #2
So, New South Wales wants
JobKeeper reinstated
to support workers.

Day 11 — 26 July

NSW Optimism Gone
Gladys now suggests
the lockdown could last for months,
grim realism is

taking hold matching
the public's mood. Asking Feds
for more vaccines falls

on deaf ears with the
PM saying lockdowns are
the way out of this.

His hypocrisy
is spectacular after
he criticised Dan.

ScoMo's favouring
of New South Wales during the
pandemic looks poor.

Victoria's Lockdown
Lockdown likely to
be lifted with tight public
health restrictions still.

Young Death
38-year-old
woman dies from COVID which
surprises many.

Protestors Were
a mix of far right,
conspiracy and also
libertarian

groups, and people who
feel disenfranchised by the
government, plus small

business owners and
antivaxxers, QAnon,
Trump followers and

evangelicals
with signs saying: *Jesus is
my vaccine,* plus the

anti-lockdown groups—
it was a coalition
of the desperate.

Unvaccinated Pandemic
So, will we see a
pandemic of those who are
unvaccinated?

Saving Grace
Playing violin
duets with bubble buddy
Linda has been the

most wondrous of times
during this lockdown. Our two
instruments melded

together to lift
our spirits and join with the
celestial choir.

It was comfort and
solace during a tough time,
music shone a light.

Day 12 — 27 July

11.30 a.m. Lockdown Lite
Lockdown ends in Vic.
but with some restrictions still
in place. People aren't

allowed in homes yet
because they are transmission
sites and too risky.

No Gloating?
As New South Wales has
a record day of cases,
Dan releases us

from our prisons and
says he's not *gloating* but I
think he's quietly smug.

So, We're At this Point
States don't trust the Feds
who don't trust the states who don't
trust each other—it's

everyone for them-
self, dog eat dog—trust is a
COVID casualty.

Survived It, Phew
Survived the lonely
lockdown with mind and body
intact. Praise the Lord!

Seven-Day Snap Lockdown 6.0

Premier Daniel Andrews Announces
Another Lockdown on 5 August
A Summary

Can You Believe It?!

Oh Bugger
Here we go again,
lockdown despair as we are
back in detention.

We were only one
week out of the last lockdown.
So how long this time?

We went from zero
cases to a lockdown in
24 hours!

No one's smug now as
we witness how quickly things
can turn around with

young folks at risk and
not just the old, so hence the
call to quick action.

Everything comes to
a crashing halt yet again—
work, play, music, sport.

I can't say how I
feel right now but our COVID
hopelessness hits hard.

March 2020—
we thought the plague would be done
by the year's end and

yet here we are still
grappling, but now with Delta's
deadly contagion.

We ride this wave of
the pandemic with blood, sweat
and fears for our health.

We are overwhelmed
by uncertainty fatigue—
can't plan tomorrow,

can't plan next week, can't
plan for anything, we're in
chaos as restaurants

turf their supplies and
businesses close, weddings are
shelved, birthdays cancelled,

funerals pruned and we
prepare to enter our caves
inconsolable.

Hundreds gather on
the streets, boisterous, dissenting,
lighting flares, chanting

COVID is fake! And
No more lockdown! Frustration
is boiling over.

As people grieve for
things they have lost, their fuming
anger ricochets.

As it stands now, three
quarters of Australia is
in lockdown. Unreal.

New South Wales struggles
to contain the virus and
the rising death-toll

as it becomes the
epicentre of the plague—
it's not going well.

While Melbourne's racked up
over 200 days of
lockdown since last year.

Life is difficult
with harsh rules and a curfew,
our movements stifled.

It is hard to stay
buoyant when you are swamped by
the pandemic's sludge.

And the 'snap lockdown'
is not just seven days, it's
never-ending weeks!

Delta's the winner—
Gladys ran up the white flag,
Dan's thrown in the towel.

Ironically Dan
and Gladys are on the same
page, abandoning

zero cases quest,
sounding more like Morrison
as the plague rolls on.

We're told we have to
learn to live with the virus
as it invades us.

Our hopes lie with the
vaccines which, sadly, were not
on offer last year.

It's biblical here
in Melbourne—plague, rioting
and Mother Earth quaked.

We are on our knees,
the foundations are crumbling
while our hope teeters.

And then suddenly
the epicentre of the
plague shifts back to us!

Melbourne bears the brunt
yet again, we're stunned mullets,
brushing tears from eye.

We wonder: will this
never end, will we ever
feel 'normal' again?

Give me my COVID
comfort food, comfort music,
comfort poetry.

And into lockdown …

---

30 September 2021 was day 56 of Lockdown 6.0
with at least another month of lockdown ahead.

>   Lockdown 1: 43 days
>   Lockdown 2: 111 days
>   Lockdown 3: 5 days
>   Lockdown 4: 14 days
>   Lockdown 5: 12 days
>   Lockdown 6: 56 days and counting …

List of Names and Terms

Federal Politicians

ScoMo/Scotty – Scott Morrison, Prime Minister, Liberal Party of Australia

Josh – Josh Frydenberg, Treasurer, Liberal Party of Australia

Greg Hunt – Minister for Health, Liberal Party of Australia

Albo – Anthony Albanese, Leader of the Opposition, Australian Labor Party

Pauline Hanson – Senator, Leader of Pauline Hanson's One Nation Party

Dan Tehan – Minister for Trade, Tourism and Investment, Liberal Party of Australia

Victorian State Politicians

Dan – Daniel Andrews, Premier of the State of Victoria, Australian Labor Party

James Merlino – Deputy Premier, Australian Labor Party

Tim Pallas – Treasurer, Australian Labor Party

Jenny Mikakos – Minister for Health until 26 September 2020, Australian Labor Party

Martin Foley – Minister for Health from 26 September 2020, Australian Labor Party

Michael O'Brien – Leader of the Opposition until 8 September 2021, Liberal Party of Australia

Matthew Guy – Leader of the Opposition from 8 September 2021, Liberal Party of Australia

Fiona Patten – Leader of the Reason Party, Member of the Victorian Legislative Council

Other State Politicians

Gladys Berejiklian – Premier of New South Wales, Liberal Party of Australia

Annastacia Palaszczuk – Premier of Queensland, Australian Labor Party

Deb Frecklington – Leader of the Queensland Opposition and Leader of the Liberal National Party of Queensland (LNP) until 12 November 2020

New Zealand

Jacinda Ardern – Prime Minister of New Zealand, New Zealand Labour Party

Other Terms

ABC – Australian Broadcasting Corporation

Ablett Senior – Gary Ablett, former Australian Rules Footballer and father of footballer Gary Ablett Junior

Across the ditch – the Tasman Sea between Australia and New Zealand

ACT – Australian Capital Territory

ADF – Australian Defence Force

AFL – Australian Football League

Andrew Bolt – conservative commentator, newspaper columnist and broadcaster

Apollo Bay – Coastal town in Victoria

ASX – The Australian Securities Exchange

Box Hill – Melbourne suburb

Brisbane – Capital of Queensland

Brownlow – Brownlow Medal awarded to the best and fairest player in the AFL

Bunnings – Large retail chain of hardware stores, famous for the weekend sausage sizzles held by community groups as fundraisers

Casey – Local government area of Melbourne

Cathy – Cathy Freeman, Indigenous athlete, Olympic Gold medallist Sydney 2000

The Cats – Geelong Football Club

CBT – Cognitive Behavioural Therapy

CFA – Country Fire Authority

Chadstone Shopping Centre (colloquially known as **Chaddy**) – large shopping centre located in Melbourne

Charlie – nickname for the Brownlow Medal

CHO – Chief Health Officer

Chooks – Colloquial term for chickens

CHOPS – Christmas Hills Orchestral Players

Chris Eccles – Head of the Department of Premier and Cabinet in Victoria until October 2020

Chrissy Hills – Christmas Hills, a rural community in Melbourne's north

The Dees – Melbourne Football Club known as the Demons

Dr Nick Coatsworth – Deputy Chief Medical Officer, infectious diseases specialist

ECT – Electroconvulsive Therapy

FLOTUS – First Lady of the United States

Frankston – Melbourne bayside suburb

Gabba – The Brisbane Cricket Ground in Woolloongabba

Geelong – Regional city, Victoria

Gerry Harvey – Executive chairman of Harvey Norman

GF – Grand Final

GOP – Grand Old Party, The Republican Party

Hallam – Melbourne suburb

Harvey Norman – Retailer of furniture, computers and electrical products

James McCaw – Professor of Mathematical Biology at the University of Melbourne

Jeff Kennett – The 43rd Premier of Victoria from 1992–1999

Jeroen Weimar – Victoria's Commander, COVID-19 Response, Department of Health

JobKeeper – Wages payment subsidy scheme for businesses affected by coronavirus (COVID-19).

JobMaker – Hiring incentive to encourage businesses to employ young jobseekers

JobSeeker – Unemployment payment scheme, boosted during the pandemic.

John Farnham – Australian entertainer

Journo Swan – Jonathan Swan, an Australian journalist who works as a political reporter for Axio, son of Norman

Julian Assange – editor, publisher, and founder of WikiLeaks in 2006

Keynes – John Maynard, English economist whose ideas fundamentally changed the theory and practice of macroeconomics and the economic policies of governments

Kilmore – Regional city, Victoria

Kiwis – New Zealanders

Larundel – Larundel Psychiatric Hospital

Lieutenant General John Frewen – COVID-19 task force commander

Lion King Neale – Lachie Neale who plays for the Brisbane Lions in the AFL, winner of the Brownlow Medal in 2020

Magda – Magda Szubanski, Australian comedian and celebrity

MCG – Melbourne Cricket Ground affectionately known as the 'G'

Melbourne – Capital of Victoria

Melbourne Cup – Australia's most famous horse race held on the first Tuesday in November at Flemington Racecourse

Melbourne Storm – the Melbourne-based rugby club in the NRL

Menzies – Sir Robert Menzies, Australian politician who twice served as Prime Minister of Australia, in office from 1939 to 1941 and again from 1949 to 1966. He played a central role in the creation of the Liberal Party of Australia.

Mike Baird – Former politician, the 44th Premier of New South Wales, Liberal Party of Australia

MSO – Melbourne Symphony Orchestra

Myer – Department store

NDE – Near Death Experience

NHS – National Health Service, the publicly funded healthcare system of the United Kingdom

Norman Swan – physician, journalist and broadcaster

Northcote – Melbourne suburb

NRL – National Rugby League

NSW – New South Wales

Pat Cash – Australian tennis player who won the Wimbledon singles title in 1987

Penrith Panthers – a rugby club in the NRL

Peta Credlin – Australian political commentator, Chief of Staff to former Prime Minister Tony Abbott

The Pies – Collingwood Football Club known as the Magpies

PM – Prime Minister

Poh Ling Yeow – a Malaysian-born Australian cook, artist, actress, author and television presenter

POTUS – President of the United States

Professor Brendan Crabb – infectious disease researcher with a special interest in malaria

Professor Brett Sutton – Victoria's Chief Health Officer

QAnon or Q – Far right conspiracy theorist group

Quaddie – betting term for picking four winners

Ruth Bader Ginsburg – Former Associate Justice of the Supreme Court of the United States

SA – South Australia

Sophie Black – Australian journalist

Spotlight – Store selling fabric, craft, party, home interiors, curtains,

Sydney – Capital of New South Wales

Tassie – Tasmania

The Tigers – Richmond Football Club

Tony Abbott – 28th Prime Minister of Australia from 2013–2015, Leader of the Liberal Party 2009–2015

VCAL – Victorian Certificate of Applied Learning

VCE – Victorian Certificate of Education, certificate awarded on completion of secondary education

Vic. – Victoria

Waleed Aly – Australian writer, academic, lawyer, and broadcaster

Wild West – Western Australia

*If you would like to know more about Spinifex Press,
write to us for a free catalogue, visit our website
and subscribe to our monthly newsletter.*

Spinifex Press
PO Box 105
Mission Beach QLD 4852
Australia

www.spinifexpress.com.au
women@spinifexpress.com.au